The Cost of
THE CALL

Finding Healing from PTSD in Christ

DAVID MENDOZA III

www.booksforhisglory.com

The Cost of THE CALL
Finding Healing from PTSD in Christ

ISBN Hardcover: 979-8-9954599-0-3
ISBN Paperback: 979-8-9933809-9-5
ISBN eBook: 979-8-9954599-1-0

First Edition: May 2026

Printed in the United States of America

DEDICATION

To all first responders and veterans who sacrifice pieces of themselves each day for the safety of others—from the streets of our cities to the dirt roads of our counties, from securing our borders to the emergency rooms and the unseen battlefields—thank you for your service. May the Lord grant you the peace your soul has been searching for, the rest your spirit deserves, and the healing only He can give.

AUTHOR'S DISCLAIMER

The content presented in this book is based on personal experience, spiritual reflection, and years of service working alongside veterans and first responders. I am not a licensed clinician, psychologist, psychiatrist, or medical professional. The information shared in these pages should not be interpreted as professional medical or psychological advice, diagnosis, or treatment.

My perspective comes from my personal journey as a military veteran and first responder who has experienced the effects of trauma and post-traumatic stress. In addition, my insights are shaped by my work serving others as a chaplain, peer support member, and participant in veteran support programs within the federal government. I also write from my experience as a Christian minister and pastor, offering spiritual encouragement grounded in faith and biblical principles.

The purpose of this book is to provide encouragement, hope, and perspective for those who may be facing similar struggles. While many of the topics discussed involve trauma, healing, and emotional well-being, readers should understand that this book is not intended to replace professional counseling, therapy, or medical treatment.

If you are experiencing symptoms related to trauma, post-traumatic stress, depression, anxiety, or any other mental health concern, it is strongly recommended that you seek assistance from qualified healthcare professionals, licensed counselors, or mental health specialists.

My hope is that the stories, reflections, and spiritual principles shared in this book will encourage readers to pursue healing, seek support when needed, and find strength in faith and community.

No two journeys toward healing are exactly the same. This book simply reflects one path—a path shaped by personal experience, faith, and a desire to help others know that they are not alone.

CONTENTS

THE CALL

"For I know the plans I have for you, declares the Lord, plans to prosper you and not to harm you, plans to give you hope and a future."

JEREMIAH 29:11

Being a first responder isn't just a job—it's a calling. Like most callings from God, it doesn't always come wrapped in comfort or clarity. Sometimes it comes quietly, as a pull on your heart you can't explain. Other times it shows up loud and unmistakable, demanding that you step forward when others step back.

The Cost of THE CALL
Finding Healing from PTSD in Christ

When people inquire about the meaning of the term "first responder," they often expect a concise definition—titles, departments, insignia. Yet such descriptions, while accurate, feel incomplete. A first responder is not defined solely by uniform or rank, but by response. It is the individual who moves toward chaos while others seek distance from it. It is the man or woman who arrives on the most devastating day of another person's life and chooses to remain present.

Some of us wore badges. Others wore military gear. Some carried medical equipment, radios, or rifles. Some never left a dispatch console, yet absorbed every cry for help, every fractured sentence, every final farewell long after the line disconnected. Others served in combat zones, along borders, inside emergency departments, or in environments where suffering became routine. Though the uniforms varied, the burden did not.

Few enter this vocation by accident. There is typically an internal conviction—a desire to serve, to shield, to intervene—that precedes formal training. It is a disposition that resists passivity. Many first responders I have known exhibited this inclination long before they were sworn in or deployed. They were not content with self-preservation alone. They sensed a summons toward something greater, even if they did not yet comprehend the full cost attached to it.

And there is, undeniably, a cost.

WHEN THE COST BECOMES A WOUND

For many years, I believed the cost of the call was limited to exhaustion and sacrifice—missed milestones, disrupted routines, strained relationships. I told myself that such losses were simply the price of service. If I remained strong enough, disciplined enough, faithful enough, I could absorb it. But some costs do not remain visible. Some costs descend beneath the surface.

Initially, their presence is subtle. You attribute the heaviness to fatigue. To stress. To adjustment. You continue forward because that is what you were trained to do. First responders do not pause; we proceed. We compartmentalize and advance to the next call. Yet while we move on from the scene, the scene does not move on from us.

Images persist. Faces reappear uninvited. Sounds replay in the stillness of night. Sleep becomes fragmented, shallow, or avoided altogether. Though physically present in the room, the mind remains elsewhere—revisiting a decision, a moment, an outcome that cannot be reversed.

It is in this environment that Post-Traumatic Stress Disorder begins to take root—not as evidence of frailty, but as the accumulated residue of repeated exposure to trauma. The nervous system remains vigilant long after the shift concludes. The body and brain continue to operate as though danger is imminent, even when the threat has passed.

For many of us, however, the injury extends beyond the psychological. At some point, the burden becomes spiritual. Questions emerge—questions long deferred. Where was God in that moment? Why was intervention absent? Why did one life end while another was spared? Why was I required to make a decision that would alter lives forever?

This is spiritual injury: the gradual erosion of faith when lived experience appears inconsistent with belief. It is not rebellion, nor is it indifference. It is the soul straining to reconcile suffering it was never designed to shoulder alone.

There is also a wound less frequently acknowledged, even within faith communities: moral injury.

Moral injury arises from actions taken—or witnessed—that conflict with one's deepest convictions. Decisions rendered in seconds that reverberate for decades. Orders executed. Force applied. Assistance that arrived too late. Outcomes beyond one's control that nonetheless feel personally borne.

Such wounds penetrate beyond cognition. They reach into identity. Into vocation. Into the understanding of who one believed himself to be and who he believed God had called him to become.

When these injuries remain unnamed and untreated, isolation follows. We distance ourselves from others, convinced they cannot comprehend the weight. We distance ourselves from God, uncertain whether He comprehends it either.

This is where many first responders and veterans quietly stand—exhausted, wounded, still committed to service, yet inwardly unraveling. Faithful, yet conflicted. Functioning, yet fractured.

I know this terrain intimately. While certain scars may never disappear entirely, I have come to understand this: healing remains possible. Not through denial. Not through suppression. But through Christ meeting us within the brokenness and teaching us to bear it differently.

This work does not promise an immediate remedy. It invites a journey—from calling, through cost, into the interior battle—and toward the discovery that even in these depths, God is not absent.

He never was.

SEPERATING THE PAIN

When I first entered law enforcement, an uncle of mine—who had worn the badge for most of his adult life—pulled me aside to offer a final word of counsel. He looked at me with the seriousness of a man who had seen much and said, "Son, remember this: leave work at work, and leave home at home." I nodded as though I understood. In truth, I did not.

The advice sounded simple, even reasonable. With time, however, I discovered how extraordinarily difficult it was to practice. No academy course teaches you how to leave the images behind. No field training officer explains how to silence the echoes of what you have witnessed once the shift ends. Work does not remain neatly confined to a patrol car. It follows you. It settles into your thoughts. It revisits you in quiet moments and refuses dismissal.

Call after call, the accumulation began. Scenes I entered. Voices I heard. Decisions I was required to make in seconds that would linger for years. I reassured myself that I was managing it well. I believed I was steady. Yet gradually—and almost imperceptibly—I began carrying that weight home.

Its effects surfaced first in subtle ways. In my marriage. In my interactions with my children. I was physically present, yet emotionally withdrawn. My patience shortened. My responses dulled. When guilt over that distance accompanied me back to work, it compromised my focus there as well.

Eventually, the boundaries dissolved altogether. I could no longer distinguish clearly between occupational pressure and personal strain. Stress, once manageable, intensified into something overwhelming. What began as a steady current became a tidal force, and in time it crashed against every area of my life.

Unable to confront it directly, I responded as many in my position do: I immersed myself more deeply in the profession. The uniform became a sanctuary. The job provided structure, clarity, and measurable outcomes. It felt safer to run toward chaos in the street than to face quiet tension at home.

What I did not recognize then was that the strain did not originate solely in law enforcement. I was also carrying unresolved wounds from my military service—experiences and internal conflicts for which I lacked vocabulary. Trauma layered upon trauma. Pressures compounded rather than dissipated.

The more determined I was to manage it alone, the more unmanageable it became.

Eventually, I turned to an escape that required no explanation: alcohol.

Drinking offered temporary silence. It slowed racing thoughts. It blurred the dividing line between work and home when I no longer possessed the discipline to separate them. Within our circle, we even gave it a harmless-sounding label— "choir practice."

Several of us would gather, sometimes in remote areas, sometimes at someone's residence. We often designated a driver—our so-called "double-D." If that plan failed, we simply remained where we were until the following morning. We reassured ourselves that it was structured, responsible, contained. In reality, it intensified the problem.

For brief intervals, alcohol resembled relief. It imitated peace. Yet quietly and persistently, it eroded what little equilibrium remained. Drinking was not merely tolerated within the culture; it was normalized. It became an unofficial coping strategy—an accepted method of survival.

In those years, few departments offered peer-support programs or accessible chaplaincy services. Conversations about trauma were rare. Emotional vulnerability was discouraged. We managed distress as we had been trained in the military: by suppressing it.

To acknowledge emotional pain was to risk being labeled weak—weak-minded, weak-hearted. And weakness, we believed, was incompatible with the profession. So silence prevailed, even as many of us struggled privately.

The consequences, however, surfaced regardless. Divorces became common. Driving under the influence charges increased. Incidents of public intoxication occurred with troubling frequency. Most devastating of all were the suicides—colleagues whose names we knew, whose faces we recognized, whose funerals we attended in solemn quiet.

During my early years, there existed what was informally referred to as "courtesy of the badge." If an officer encountered another officer who had been drinking, it was not unusual for the matter to be resolved discreetly—a ride home, a call to a trusted friend.

For someone young and inexperienced, that practice fostered a dangerous illusion. I was convinced, at times, that I was untouchable. Indestructible.

That illusion did not endure. Departments gradually tightened policies. Informal courtesies diminished. Arrests replaced warnings. Some agencies adopted uncompromising disciplinary measures.

These changes were signals—evidence that a deeper issue was unfolding within the profession. Yet we lacked the framework to address the root cause. We treated visible behaviors while neglecting the underlying wound.

For me, this period marked only the beginning of a far more personal reckoning.

GETTING IN DEEPER

My drinking didn't just get worse—it became normal. What once felt excessive gradually became routine. Over time, we stopped identifying it as a problem at all. The strain, the heaviness, the quiet desperation—these were simply accepted as occupational hazards. If you intended to survive in this profession, you absorbed the cost without complaint. You learned to suppress the discomfort, to compartmentalize the pain, to function around the fracture.

Only in hindsight can I see the truth. We were not simply coping; we were anesthetizing. Call after call, shift after shift, we muted portions of our humanity in order to endure what confronted us daily. It was not a conscious decision so much as an adaptation. We shut down what felt unbearable so we could continue to perform.

We did not use clinical terms such as *trauma* or *post-traumatic stress* in those days. Yet that is precisely what we were carrying. We absorbed violence, grief, and chaos with no structured or safe means of release. Under sustained stress, the human body and mind will adapt in order to survive. That adaptation, however necessary, exacts a cost.

We grew emotionally hardened. Detached. Not because we lacked compassion, but because unfiltered empathy would have overwhelmed us. Numbness became our armor. It shielded us in moments of crisis. It enabled us to walk into scenes others could not endure. Yet what protected us operationally endangered us personally.

We constructed walls thick enough to withstand anything. Those walls served us on the street. They preserved composure and sharpened focus. What we failed to recognize was that we did not dismantle them when we returned home. We convinced ourselves we were shielding our families from the darkness we witnessed. In reality, we no longer knew how to lower the defenses without risking collapse.

Within my own home, those defenses altered the character of my marriage. My wife and I ceased functioning as partners and gradually became cohabitants. We occupied the same physical space yet inhabited separate emotional worlds. Warmth gave way to distance. Intimacy yielded to silence. The connection that once defined us diminished quietly, replaced by a tension neither of us fully understood.

That emotional detachment made us highly effective in crisis. We remained composed under pressure. We entered volatile environments without hesitation. In many respects, we excelled professionally. Yet the very traits that enhanced performance undermined presence. We were trained to manage chaos, not cultivate closeness.

To be candid, some degree of psychological protection was necessary. No individual is designed to witness repeated violence, death, abuse, and despair without consequence. First responders encounter humanity at its most fractured—tragedy in its rawest expression. Exposure of that magnitude inevitably leaves residue.

The question rarely posed is this: what becomes of that residue when the shift concludes? Where does the accumulated grief, adrenaline, and hypervigilance go once the uniform is removed? What occurs when the nervous system remains activated long after the immediate threat has passed?

How does sustained exposure to trauma reshape a person emotionally, physically, and spiritually? What are the long-term effects of compressing pain year after year, addressing symptoms while neglecting the underlying wound? Healing cannot begin where acknowledgment is absent.

For me, restoration required more than discipline. It required more than determination, more than distraction, more than another drink at the end of a long shift. It required intervention beyond my own capacity to engineer. Even then, I did not recognize it for what it was.

Before any meaningful healing could occur, I had to confront a difficult truth: I was no longer managing the strain. I was confined by it. What I had once called coping had quietly become captivity.

TRAPPED

From the outside, everything appeared fine. People saw the patrol car, the pressed uniform, the polished badge. They saw what looked like a respectable profession—authority, purpose, stability. What they could not see was what unfolded behind the curtain.

They did not hear the constant noise in my mind or feel the pressure that lived in my chest. They did not see how thin the line had become between composure and collapse. On the surface, I functioned. Beneath it, there was no peace—only unrest carefully concealed beneath discipline and routine.

At home, my wife and I had become strangers sharing the same address. Conversation often deteriorated into conflict. When we were not arguing, we were silent. The spaces that once held warmth and laughter were now filled with tension and exhaustion. Love had not vanished, but it was buried under layers of resentment, disappointment, and pain neither of us knew how to articulate.

What unsettled me most was not the anger or even the distance. It was the gradual erosion of care. It did not disappear overnight. It faded quietly, almost imperceptibly.

The things that once anchored me—faith, family, meaningful relationships—drifted to the margins. In their place, distractions and escapes took priority. My sense of order inverted itself, and I lacked the awareness to recognize how profoundly my values had shifted.

There is a cruel irony in this calling. First responders are often among the most compassionate individuals one will encounter. They enter professions such as law enforcement, military service, and emergency medicine because they feel a deep, almost sacred responsibility to protect and to serve. There is within them a God-given impulse toward sacrifice.

They are loyal. Disciplined. Willing to place themselves in harm's way for people whose names they may never know.

Yet that same devotion—the very quality that makes them effective—can quietly become destructive. The commitment that strengthens their professional identity can also isolate them emotionally.

At first, the isolation feels manageable. Even safe. It provides structure. Expectations are clear. Emotions are compartmentalized. Performance replaces vulnerability. But over time, what once felt protective becomes confining. The walls narrow. The air thins. And eventually, without realizing it, one finds himself suffocating in the very space that once offered refuge.

I did not understand this dynamic in my earlier years. Only later—after becoming a born-again Christian—did I begin to perceive the deeper interplay at work.

The physical and the spiritual are not separate domains. Each informs and influences the other. Trauma affects the body, but it also burdens the soul. Spiritual disconnection shapes emotional health, which in turn manifests physically. Attempts to divide these realities inevitably fail.

I was living with a legitimate mental and physical strain produced by years of cumulative trauma—from both military service and law enforcement. Yet beneath the surface, something more profound was unraveling. My spirit was weary. My faith was obscured by shame, unanswered questions, and unprocessed grief.

Physically, I could not see a path forward. Emotionally, I felt isolated. Spiritually, I felt distant from the very foundation I once claimed.

I attempted conversation with colleagues, hoping shared experience might provide clarity. It did not. I attempted conversation with my wife, hoping honesty might restore connection. It often deepened the divide. We were all wounded in different ways, yet none of us possessed the language or tools necessary to address the depth of what was happening.

One of the most difficult lessons I have learned is this: one cannot give what one does not possess.

My partners could not offer what they themselves had never been shown. My wife could not articulate insights she had not been equipped to understand. Their inability was not a failure of love. It was a limitation of formation. And I shared in that same limitation.

Something had to change. Pressure cannot increase indefinitely without consequence. Eventually, something yields.

An older manager once remarked during a particularly difficult season, "Sometimes you just have to let the bottom of the basket fall." At the time, I dismissed it as crude humor—perhaps even reckless advice. Now I recognize its meaning.

When the bottom of the basket falls, everything spills out. The carefully balanced contents scatter. What has been held together by sheer willpower collapses under its own weight. The illusion of control dissolves. Exposure becomes unavoidable.

The bottom of the basket fell. And when it did, there was no reconstructing the old structure. There was only the undeniable reality that what I had been carrying could no longer be contained.

Chapter One Reflection - *The Call*

If any part of this chapter felt familiar, you're not alone—and you're not broken.

The calling to serve often comes with a deep sense of purpose, but purpose does not make a person immune to pain. What you've read here is not a story of failure; it's a story of exposure. PTSD does not show up because you were weak—it shows up because you endured more than the human nervous system was designed to carry alone.

Many first responders and veterans live trapped between two worlds. At work, you are trained to run toward danger, suppress emotion, and stay in control. At home, you are expected to be present, gentle, and emotionally available. When trauma goes unaddressed, those two worlds collide—and something inside begins to fracture.

Numbness, anger, withdrawal, addiction, and isolation are not moral failures. They are often survival responses. But survival is not the same as healing.

This chapter is not asking you to fix anything yet. It is simply asking you to **name the cost**. To acknowledge the wounds you've been carrying. To admit—maybe for the first time—that something inside you hurts and needs attention.

God is not surprised by your pain. He is not offended by your questions. And He has not abandoned you in the middle of your struggle.

The call was real. The cost was real. And the wounds that followed are real too. But this is not where the story ends.

A Prayer for the Wounded Servant

Lord,

You see what I've carried—the calls that never left me, the weight I didn't know how to put down, the parts of myself I lost along the way.

I confess that I've been surviving instead of healing. I've built walls to protect myself, and those same walls have kept others—and You—at a distance.

I don't know how to fix what's broken inside me, but I'm willing to stop running.

Meet me here, God—in the confusion, in the exhaustion, in the fear. Give me the courage to face the truth, and the strength to take the next step.

I place this burden in Your hands, trusting that You can carry what I cannot. Amen.

Practical Takeaway - *One Step Toward Healing*

You don't need to change everything right now. You only need to take **one honest step**.

Before moving on to the next chapter, take a few moments—alone and without distractions—and ask yourself this question:

"What am I still carrying that I've never talked about?"

You don't have to share it yet. You don't have to solve it. Just name it—privately, honestly, without judgment.

If you're able, write it down. If writing feels unsafe, acknowledge it silently.

If faith feels distant, simply sit with the question.

Healing from PTSD does not begin with answers. It begins with **awareness**. And awareness is an act of courage.

The Cost of THE CALL

Finding Healing from PTSD in Christ

This area is designated for writing notes:

NO TURNING BACK

"The heart of man plans his way, but the LORD establishes his steps."

PROVERBS 16:9

There are moments in life when everything you have been holding together finally gives way. For me, that moment arrived in the form of flashing red and blue lights reflected in my rearview mirror.

I still remember the weight in my chest when I realized there would be no talking my way out of this one. No professional courtesy. No quiet warning. No ride home from a colleague who understood the culture. Only the sound of gravel beneath my tires as I pulled to the shoulder, knowing—deep down—that this was the inevitable result of choices I had been making for a long time.

This was not bad luck. This was not a misunderstanding. This was consequence.

As a first responder, I had witnessed this scene countless times from the opposite side of the driver's window. I had stood where that officer now stood. I had looked into the eyes of men and women who insisted, "This isn't who I am," even as the evidence suggested otherwise. I had listened to explanations, promises, and regret. Now I was the one sitting under the glare of emergency lights—exposed, stripped of rank, reputation, and control. The badge did not matter. The uniform did not matter. The excuses did not matter.

In that moment, I was not a law enforcement officer. I was not a Marine. I was not the disciplined professional I had worked so hard to become. I was a broken man who could no longer outrun his pain.

Shame arrived first. Not merely fear of legal repercussions, but the crushing awareness that I had crossed a line I once enforced. I had become the very cautionary tale I used to warn others about. Yet the most sobering realization was not that I had been caught; it was how far I had drifted while convincing myself that everything was still under control. This is where denial dies.

Up until that night, I had persuaded myself that I was managing it. I could stop whenever I chose. My drinking was contained. My anger was justified. My emotional distance was necessary. I believed I could continue serving, continue surviving, and somehow prevent everything from collapsing at once.

The arrest told a different story. It told the truth I had refused to confront: the old way of living was no longer sustainable.

What I did not understand at the time—what I can only recognize now in hindsight—is that this devastating moment was also mercy.

Not mercy that erased consequences. I paid for my actions. I accepted responsibility. I walked through the fallout— professionally, personally, and spiritually. Grace does not eliminate accountability. It does not shield us from the harvest of what we have sown. But mercy appeared in the exposure.

God allowed the carefully constructed façade to collapse completely. The coping mechanisms failed. The image shattered. The illusion of invulnerability dissolved. And for the first time in years, I had nowhere left to hide—behind performance, behind rank, behind alcohol, or behind pride.

That night marked the end of something. The end of pretending. The end of numbing. The end of believing I could outrun wounds I refused to heal. There was no turning back, because there was nothing left to return to.

I did not yet know what healing would require. I was not certain it was even possible. All I understood was that the road I had been traveling led only toward destruction, and remaining on it would eventually cost me everything—my career, my marriage, perhaps even someone else's life.

This chapter does not begin with redemption. It begins with exposure. Because sometimes the most loving thing God can do is stop us—decisively and without warning—before we destroy ourselves and those we love.

Sometimes the arrest is not the end of the story. It is the intervention.

YOU CAN'T HIDE

That night, sitting behind the bars of a jail cell, everything came into focus. The noise had stopped. The distractions were gone. For the first time in a long time, there was nowhere left to run. Though I was devastated, I was also confronted with a clarity I could no longer avoid—something had to change.

Stripped of the uniform, the badge, and the image I had worked so hard to maintain, I was left alone with the truth. I was not simply facing consequences; I was confronting a calling I had been resisting for years.

For nearly three years, God had been pursuing me—patiently, faithfully, relentlessly. And I had ignored Him.

Every time I walked into a bar, every time I gathered with the guys for another so-called "choir practice," I sensed His voice. It was not harsh. It was not condemning. It was steady, gentle, and unmistakable: *This is not who you are. This is not who I created you to be.*

Each time I felt that conviction, I responded the same way—I drank faster.

I chugged beer not only to numb the pain but to drown out the voice that called me higher. I did not want to feel. I did not want to listen. I certainly did not want to change. Alcohol became my method of suppression, my way of silencing conviction—at least temporarily.

It was not until I found myself sitting on that cold jail cell floor that I realized I had reached my crossroads.

In that sterile, fluorescent-lit silence, the weight of reality settled in. I was on the brink of losing everything. Not just my job—my identity. Law enforcement was more than a career; it was who I believed myself to be. It was what I lived for, trained for, sacrificed for.

My marriage was already fragile. I was battling inner demons daily—trauma, anger, shame, exhaustion. But the possibility of losing the one thing I believed defined me finally pierced the walls I had built around my heart.

I had been running for a long time. Now I was confined to a space where running was no longer an option. You cannot hide from God—not because He seeks to punish, but because He loves too deeply to leave you unchanged.

This arrest was not something God inflicted upon me. It was the natural consequence of my own choices. I bore full responsibility. Accountability is painful, but it is also honest.

The following morning, I did what integrity required. I called my supervisor and explained exactly what had happened. His response stunned me. His primary concern was whether I still had a valid driver's license and whether I would take care of the citation.

In those days, in certain circles, a DWI arrest was treated almost as a rite of passage—an unofficial initiation into a fraternity of shared recklessness.

When I walked into the station, I braced myself for termination. Instead, I was met with jokes, congratulations, and welcomes to the "club" from senior officers and supervisors.

On the surface, it seemed normal—almost celebratory. Inside, it felt deeply wrong.

I knew that if nothing changed, I would eventually destroy myself—or worse, someone else. The weight of that realization pressed heavily on me. I had taken an oath to serve and protect. In my heart, I believed I had dishonored that oath. Shame and guilt settled in, not as fleeting emotions but as sobering truth.

After months of stress and significant legal expenses, my attorney succeeded in having the charge reduced to reckless driving. Legally, that outcome brought relief. Spiritually, however, the damage had already exposed deeper fractures. The "black eye" remained—not on my record alone, but on my conscience. And it forced a reckoning.

One evening, while walking into the station, I noticed a book lying nearby: *The God Chasers* by Tommy Tenney. A friend had been reading it. I asked whether it was worth my time. Without hesitation, he handed it to me and said, "Take it—I'm finished."

That simple exchange became a turning point.

Through that book, I sensed God speaking directly into my life. I devoured it in three days. For the first time in years, my heart felt awake rather than numb. Conviction no longer felt like condemnation; it felt like an invitation.

I did not stop drinking immediately, but I learned a decisive lesson. From that day forward, I never again drank and drove.

Over the next three months, I became intensely hungry for God. I sought Him with a desperation I could not ignore. I wanted more of Him; I simply did not know how to pursue Him fully.

As a child, my grandmother—an unwavering believer—had occasionally taken me to church. She was the first person to teach me about God. When I was eleven years old, I attended a service where the preacher's message stirred something deep within me. When he gave an altar call, I ran forward and dedicated my life to God.

Somewhere along the way, however, I drifted. I chose independence over surrender. I would attend church sporadically—even during Marine Corps boot camp, when some of us marched to services more for a break from the grind than for worship. God was familiar, but distant.

Then came a morning when I could no longer ignore the internal collapse. Driving to work, I felt utterly depleted—physically, mentally, emotionally, and spiritually. I could not sustain the pace. I could not maintain the façade.

I pulled over on the side of Highway 44, activated my hazard lights, and sat alone in my patrol car. And for the first time in years, I stopped running. I closed my eyes and spoke honestly.

"God, I know You're real. I do not fully understand Christianity, but if You can use this mess—here I am. I give it all to You."

In that moment, something shifted inside of me. On the outside, the circumstances remained unchanged. My marriage was still strained, my career was unstable, the consequences still loomed. But internally, a burden lifted. The striving quieted.

God met me there—on the side of the road, not in a sanctuary, not before a pastor or priest, just me and Him, alone. He found me, broken, exposed and finally willing. That was not merely a moment of reflection. It was a decision.

NOW OR NEVER

There are moments in life when a single decision divides your story into *before* and *after*. This was one of those moments. When I surrendered my life to Christ on the side of Highway 44, I knew it was not emotional hype. It was not merely desperation after a difficult season. It was a deliberate line drawn in the sand. I understood, even then, that this decision would touch every part of my life—my marriage, my career, my friendships, my identity. It was a crossroads. It was now or never.

What I did not anticipate was that obedience would initially make everything harder.

All day I had waited for the right moment to tell my wife. I was genuinely excited. I believed she would see what I felt—that something real had shifted inside me. I imagined relief, maybe even hope. To me, this was good news.

Instead, when I finished explaining that I had given my heart to Jesus and intended to live differently, she looked at me calmly and said she wanted a divorce.

Her reasoning was painfully logical. If we struggled when we were "the same," she said, how could we possibly make it work now that I had changed?

Her words crushed me. Yet beneath the sting, I recognized a difficult truth: this was my decision. I had chosen this path freely. I could not—and would not—force it upon her. Just as no one had coerced me into surrendering my life to God, I could not manipulate her into faith. Love does not operate by pressure. It cannot be engineered.

We agreed to continue living together, but we existed more as roommates than as husband and wife. The distance remained. The wounds were still tender. The difference now was that I had chosen a new direction—even if I appeared to be walking it alone.

During that season, I remember asking God repeatedly, *How do I convince her? How do I get her to come to church? How do I bring her with me?*

The answer that settled in my spirit was simple and unsettling: "Just love her. No matter what."

I pushed back internally. *No matter what, Lord?*

Again, the response: "No matter what."

That kind of love did not come naturally to me. It had to be learned. It had to be formed in me. Loving without conditions. Loving without expecting immediate change. Loving even when the affection did not seem to be returned.

Slowly—almost imperceptibly—something began to shift. The change was not dramatic. There were no grand speeches or sudden reconciliations. It was steady and quiet. My wife began to notice something different in me—something that could not be manufactured. A peace that did not match our circumstances. A patience that had replaced defensiveness. A humility that had not existed before.

Months later, one evening while we sat together in the living room, she asked me, "How do I get what you have?"

I told her it was not something you earn. It is something you receive. You ask God into your life, and He begins the work.

The following Sunday, she attended church with me. A few weeks later, she made her own decision to surrender her life to Christ.

It remains one of the happiest moments of my life—not because I had won an argument, not because I had persuaded her, but because it was authentic. It was her choice. Her surrender.

Our marriage did not transform overnight. Trust had to be rebuilt. Old patterns had to be dismantled. Healing, like faith, is a process. But this time we were no longer fighting from opposite corners. We were learning to stand side by side.

If you ask my wife today what drew her to Christ, she will tell you it was not perfection or preaching. It was authenticity. It was love.

Looking back, our journey has not been easy. We have faced challenges like any couple. The difference now is that we do not face them alone. We no longer battle each other; we battle together.

Changes followed me into the workplace as well. When I chose to follow Christ openly, some friendships quietly dissolved. The barbecues stopped. The "choir practices" faded. Invitations slowed until they disappeared altogether.

I did not make a public announcement, nor did I distance myself intentionally. But when your values change, your environment inevitably responds. Walking with God sometimes means walking through seasons of isolation.

Yet I learned something powerful during that time: when you walk with Christ, you are never truly alone. Before Him, I could stand in a room full of people and feel empty. With Him, even solitude felt full.

As the months passed, another desire began to stir within me—a renewed longing to help others. I had always been drawn to service. That is why I joined the military. That is why I became a first responder. But this felt different. This was not about adrenaline or identity. It was about purpose.

I could recognize the darkness in some of my partners' lives because I had lived there. I saw the signs—the drinking, the anger, the withdrawal. I wanted to help, but I did not know how.

Then one evening, as I walked into the station, a supervisor stopped me and said, "Hey, aren't you a Christian now?"

I laughed. "Yes, sir."

"They just announced a chaplain position at sector. Would you be interested?"

Would I ever.

Within weeks, I became an official chaplain for my agency. Never in a million years would I have imagined that path for myself. I have often thought that God has a remarkable sense of humor.

By nature, I am an introvert. As a child, words had to be drawn out of me. Looking back now, I sometimes wonder if God was simply preserving my voice for a different season.

I served as a chaplain for several years. Later, when our agency launched a Peer Support Program, I was asked to participate. Eventually, I also became part of a Veterans Support Program.

Through those roles, I walked alongside partners and families facing loss, depression, PTSD, suicide attempts, and crises of faith. I sat in hospital rooms. I made death notifications. I prayed with officers who believed they were beyond redemption.

I was helping others find light in their darkness.

But here is the truth: even while I was serving, even while I was praying for others, even while I carried the title of chaplain—I was still fighting my own battle.

COMMITTED

Soon after dedicating my life to Christ, I seriously contemplated resigning from law enforcement and entering into full-time ministry. The call to serve God and serve others felt unmistakable. After years of running, I wanted to give Him everything—immediately and without reservation. In my mind, leaving my badge behind seemed like the most radical and sincere act of obedience I could offer.

Yet through prayer and quiet reflection, I sensed God redirecting me—not away from law enforcement, but back into it. The message was clear: *Stay.* Over time I came to understand that surrender does not always mean walking away. Sometimes it means remaining exactly where you are and allowing God to transform the mission field you already inhabit. God will use anything we are willing to place in His hands—even a patrol car, a uniform, and a past marked by failure.

I committed myself fully. I served passionately as a chaplain, a peer support member, and later as part of the Veterans Support Program within my department. In addition, during my off-duty hours, I pastored a small church. I was driven by a deep hunger to help others, to stand beside first responders and their families during moments of crisis, grief, and uncertainty. I wanted to be the steady presence I had once needed myself.

What most people did not know, however, was that I carried a hidden struggle. Behind the sermons, the counseling sessions, and the prayers for others, I harbored a dark and persistent battle within my own mind. I felt ashamed of it. At times I wondered whether I was a hypocrite—how could I minister to others while privately wrestling with my own unresolved trauma?

Throughout my service in the department's resiliency programs—and even during my years as a pastor—I was still suffering from post-traumatic stress disorder. My faith was real. My calling was genuine. But so was the trauma.

Even years later, I cannot walk into a room without instinctively scanning for exits and positioning myself with my back to the wall. Hypervigilance became second nature. Anxiety would surface without warning. Nightmares revisited scenes I wished I could forget. For a season, depression settled in heavily, clouding my thoughts and draining my strength. These were not signs of weak faith; they were the lingering effects of cumulative trauma—of calls answered, scenes witnessed, and emotions suppressed for the sake of survival.

I often reflected on the words of the Apostle Paul in *2 Corinthians 12:8–9*. Paul pleaded with God three times to remove what he described as a "thorn in the flesh." Whatever that affliction was, it tormented him. Yet the Lord's reply was not removal but reassurance: "My grace is sufficient for you, for my power is made perfect in weakness." Paul concluded that he would boast all the more gladly about his weaknesses, so that Christ's power might rest upon him.

The Cost of THE CALL
Finding Healing from PTSD in Christ

There are prayers that seem to go unanswered—or at least unanswered in the way we desire. This is where faith is refined. Faith is not merely belief when outcomes align with our expectations; it is trust when they do not. Would I trust God even if the nightmares persisted? Would I trust Him when anxiety tightened its grip? These were not abstract theological questions. They were deeply personal.

Living with PTSD forced me to depend on God for peace in a way comfort never could. Over time, I began to see that my condition, while painful, did not disqualify me from ministry—it shaped it. The Apostle Paul's testimony taught me that weakness, surrendered to God, becomes a platform for His strength. Rather than allowing PTSD to silence me, I learned to let it inform my compassion. I could sit with a struggling officer and genuinely say, "I understand," not as a cliché, but as lived experience.

Helping others became, in many ways, my medicine. The more I committed myself to serving those who were hurting, the less power isolation had over me. Yet I also learned an important lesson: service cannot be a substitute for healing. For a time, my unresolved trauma cost me opportunities—both professionally and personally. When I gave in to fear or withdrew emotionally, it took more than I intended to surrender. PTSD is like that; the more ground you yield, the more it attempts to claim.

But I also discovered something else. The closer I walked with Christ, the more I experienced a peace that defied explanation. It did not always remove the symptoms, but it anchored me in the midst of them. My circumstances did not instantly change; my nervous system did not immediately reset. Yet I was no longer fighting alone.

Commitment, I learned, is not a one-time decision. It is daily. It is choosing to stay present when your mind wants to escape. It is choosing to trust when your body remains on alert. It is choosing to serve, to seek help when necessary, and to refuse shame's lie that you are broken beyond repair.

I was committed—to Christ, to my calling, and to the slow, often painful journey of healing. And though I was helping others find hope, I was also learning, step by step, how to find it for myself.

NOT PERFECT

None of us entered this world unmarked by brokenness. Scripture teaches that through the fall in the Garden of Eden, sin became part of the human condition. That inheritance is not merely theological language; it is the explanation for why we struggle, why we fail, and why perfection forever eludes us.

Sin is the fracture in the foundation of humanity. It is the reason our minds wrestle, our bodies weaken, and our souls ache. The apostle Paul reminds us that our true citizenship is in heaven, and that one day Christ will transform our lowly body to be like His glorious body (Phil. 3:20–21). Until that day, we live in bodies and minds that are not yet fully restored.

God has never called us to achieve perfection in our own strength. That burden would crush us. Only God is perfect. That is precisely why we need a Savior—One who was without sin, who lived the life we could not live, and who died the death we deserved. Jesus Christ did not come to enhance our self-sufficiency; He came to rescue us from it. The cross stands as both an indictment of human brokenness and a declaration of divine mercy.

This truth matters profoundly for those who serve in professions saturated with trauma. A person who works for years in environments filled with violence, tragedy, loss, and human suffering will be affected. It is not a question of weakness; it is a matter of exposure. The nervous system was not designed to absorb relentless crisis without consequence. Repeated activation of the fight-or-flight response leaves an imprint. Post-traumatic stress is not evidence of moral failure or deficient character. It is often the natural response of a body and mind that have endured more than they were created to carry alone.

For too long, first responders and veterans have carried an unnecessary layer of shame alongside their trauma. They have wondered why they cannot "shake it off," why sleep will not come, why anger rises too quickly, or why silence feels unbearable. Many have concluded—wrongly—that something is fundamentally defective within them. Yet the presence of symptoms does not define the worth of the person experiencing them. Trauma is something that happened to you; it is not who you are.

Serving in roles that demand composure in chaos shapes a person in ways that are both visible and unseen. When you are required to maintain control while others are unraveling, something happens internally. You train your mind to compartmentalize. You silence emotion in order to function. You override natural responses so that you can perform your duty. Over time, that discipline becomes reflexive. It strengthens you for the moment—but it can distance you from yourself.

Then the sirens stop. The radios fall silent. The deployment ends. The shift is over. And in that stillness, an unexpected emptiness surfaces. Many first responders learn not merely to endure chaos but to thrive in it. Adrenaline becomes familiar.

Urgency provides structure. In crisis, you know exactly who you are and what to do. But in quiet spaces—at home, alone, without the noise—there is no script. The absence of chaos can feel disorienting, even threatening. Silence exposes what busyness conceals.

For me, this was one of the most difficult realizations. I did not know how to live outside the storm. I had become fluent in emergency, yet illiterate in peace. The quiet revealed memories I had suppressed and emotions I had postponed. It was in that uncomfortable stillness that Christ began to meet me—not with condemnation, but with patience.

What Christ did for me was not instantaneous or dramatic in the way I once imagined healing would be. He did not erase my past or remove every symptom overnight. Instead, He taught me to sit in the silence without fear. He reintroduced me to stillness as a place of communion rather than threat. In the quiet, He began to untangle what trauma had knotted inside me. Slowly, almost imperceptibly at times, the internal chaos began to yield to a steadier peace.

Healing rarely unfolds on our timetable. It is often gradual, layered, and deeply personal. There are setbacks and seasons of discouragement. Yet there is also progress—sometimes measured not in the absence of symptoms, but in the presence of hope. Remaining in Christ does not guarantee a life free from struggle; it promises that we will not face that struggle alone. Over time, as we abide in Him, what once controlled us begins to loosen its grip.

There is, however, a necessary response on our part. Transformation is not passive. We must desire change. We must be willing to step toward the One who calls us. Scripture assures us that if we draw near to God, He will draw near to us (James 4:8). That promise is not conditional upon perfection; it is extended to the willing.

God does not force His presence into our lives. Love does not coerce. We are invited to open the door, to surrender what we have tried unsuccessfully to manage on our own. When we grant Him that access—when we confess our need and relinquish control—He begins a work that reaches deeper than coping strategies. He heals from the inside out.

We are not perfect. We were never meant to be our own saviors. But we are not beyond redemption, either. For the first responder who feels fractured, ashamed, or spiritually numb, this truth stands firm: your brokenness does not disqualify you from grace. It is often the very place where grace begins.

Chapter Two Reflection – *No Turning Back*

Chapter Two is the place where denial finally collapses and

reality steps into the light. For many of us who have lived in survival mode—especially in professions built around crisis—there comes a moment when the life we built to protect ourselves can no longer hold together. The systems we relied on to cope begin to break down. The habits we justified begin to expose their true cost.

For me, that moment came through the consequences of my own choices. What once felt like control revealed itself to be captivity. The arrest was not only a legal consequence; it was a spiritual confrontation. It forced me to face the truth I had spent years avoiding—that the life I was living was no longer sustainable.

Moments like this often feel like the end of everything. Pride shatters. Reputation feels lost. The future becomes uncertain. Yet sometimes the very thing that feels like destruction is actually the beginning of rescue. When God allows the walls of our self-reliance to fall, He is not abandoning us—He is creating space for something new to begin.

Accountability is not the enemy of grace. In fact, grace often arrives through accountability. Consequences wake us up to realities we were unwilling to see. They interrupt the patterns that were slowly destroying us. What felt like humiliation can become the doorway to humility, and humility is often where true healing begins.

For the first responder, the veteran, or anyone who has learned to hide pain behind strength, Chapter Two is the moment when the mask slips. It is the realization that toughness alone cannot heal what trauma has damaged. It is the moment when survival tactics stop working and the deeper battle—the battle within—finally begins to surface.

The road forward will not be easy. Facing the truth rarely is. But there is hope hidden inside that confrontation. Because once the truth is acknowledged, healing can begin. The old life can no longer continue the way it was—and that realization, painful as it may be, is the first step toward transformation.

A Small Prayer

Lord,

You see the places in my life where I have tried to hide, cope, or control things on my own. You know the mistakes I have made and the weight I carry because of them. Today, I choose honesty over denial.

Give me the courage to face the truth about where I am and how I got here. Help me accept accountability without drowning in shame. Remind me that Your mercy is greater than my failures and that Your grace is still at work even in the middle of my consequences.

Teach me to trust You with the pieces of my life that feel

broken. Lead me out of the patterns that once controlled me and into the healing only You can provide.

Amen.

Practical Takeaway - *Start with honest self-examination.*

Healing begins when we stop pretending everything is fine. Take time this week to reflect honestly on the areas of your life where coping mechanisms may have become destructive habits. This does not mean condemning yourself; it means allowing truth to surface so change can begin.

Ask yourself three simple questions:

• What patterns in my life am I using to escape pain rather than face it?

• What consequences have those patterns created for me or the people around me?

• What would it look like to invite God into that area of my life today?

Write your answers down. Speak honestly to God about them in prayer.

The goal is not perfection—it is truth. And truth is the first step toward freedom.

The Cost of THE CALL

Finding Healing from PTSD in Christ

This area is designated for writing notes:

THE CHANGE

"I will give you a new heart and put a new spirit within you; I will remove your heart of stone and give you a heart of flesh."

EZEKIEL 36:26

The change rarely happens all at once. It does not arrive with a dramatic announcement or a moment where you suddenly realize everything about you is different. Instead, it happens slowly—quietly—little by little, almost unnoticed. Day by day, shift by shift, call by call, something inside begins to shift.

At first, the changes are subtle. A little less patience than before. A little more distance from the people you love. Sleep becomes harder to find. The world seems louder in some ways and strangely numb in others. You begin to react differently to situations that once felt normal. Yet because the transformation is gradual, it rarely raises alarms in the moment. It simply becomes the new normal.

Then one day, often years later, you look in the mirror and realize something unsettling: the person staring back at you feels unfamiliar. The face may be the same, but something deeper has shifted. The optimism that once lived there may be harder to find. The lightness you once carried may now feel replaced by a weight you cannot quite explain.

This transformation is not usually something we choose. In many ways, it is something our minds and bodies learn to do in order to survive the environments we operate in. First responders, soldiers, and those who work in constant proximity to trauma must adapt. The brain rewires itself to remain alert, to react quickly, to shut down emotion when emotion would interfere with the mission. What begins as a survival mechanism slowly becomes a way of life.

Over time, we begin to reflect the environment around us. We absorb its tension, its urgency, its darkness. The more exposure we experience, the more our internal world begins to mirror the chaos we routinely step into. Without realizing it, we become the product of the very environments we were trained to navigate.

Often, the people closest to us notice the change long before we do. Spouses see it in the distance growing between conversations. Children feel it in the short temper that seems to appear out of nowhere. Friends sense it in the silence where laughter once lived. Yet many times, those who love us the most hesitate to say anything.

Sometimes they remain silent because they are afraid of the reaction they might receive. Other times they hold onto the hope that what they are witnessing is only temporary—that it is simply a phase brought on by stress or fatigue that will soon pass. They wait patiently for the person they once knew to reappear. Unfortunately, the longer the exposure continues, the more difficult it becomes for that earlier version of ourselves to return unchanged.

Part of the challenge is that the kind of trauma experienced in these professions does not always come from a single catastrophic event. Many people are familiar with Post-Traumatic Stress Disorder (PTSD) as something that develops after one particularly horrific incident—a shooting, an explosion, a natural disaster, or a near-death experience. But for many first responders and veterans, trauma does not arrive in a single moment. It accumulates over time.

There is another form of trauma known as Complex Post-Traumatic Stress Disorder, often referred to as CPTSD. Unlike traditional PTSD, which is commonly associated with one major traumatic event, CPTSD develops after prolonged and repeated exposure to distressing situations. It is the result of living for extended periods in environments where danger, suffering, and emotional intensity are routine parts of the job.

For those working in emergency services, law enforcement, military operations, or crisis response, this exposure becomes a daily reality. Call after call brings new images, new sounds, and new decisions that must be made in seconds. Some scenes stay with you longer than others, but even the ones that fade leave behind a residue. Over months and years, those layers accumulate in ways that are difficult to measure but impossible to ignore.

Many first responders and veterans struggle to recognize this in themselves because they were never involved in one single "defining" traumatic event. They may say things like, "Nothing that bad ever happened to me," or "Other people had it worse." Because their trauma came in smaller doses over a long period of time, they may dismiss the possibility that what they are experiencing has a name.

Yet the mind does not measure trauma the way we often think it does. The brain records stress, threat, and emotional shock each time it occurs. Repeated exposure to suffering—especially when paired with the pressure to remain composed and in control—gradually begins to affect emotional regulation, thought patterns, and relationships. Over time, this can lead to feelings of detachment, persistent anxiety, negative beliefs about oneself, and difficulty connecting with others.

What makes this especially challenging is that the average person will never see the things first responders and veterans see on a regular basis. Most people go through their lives without witnessing severe violence, tragic accidents, or the raw aftermath of human suffering. For those in these professions, however, such experiences are not rare—they are part of the routine.

The human mind was never designed to repeatedly process that level of intensity without some kind of impact. Yet the expectation placed on those in these roles is often the same: adapt, overcome, and keep moving. There is rarely time to stop and process what just happened because another call is already waiting. Another crisis is already unfolding somewhere else.

In many ways, entire systems are built around training individuals to function under these conditions. Governments and institutions invest enormous resources into preparing soldiers and first responders to perform under pressure. Training is designed to sharpen reflexes, strengthen discipline, and condition the mind and body to act quickly in the middle of chaos.

This training is necessary. Without it, many lives would be lost. The ability to move toward danger when others are running away is a vital part of protecting society. But there is an uncomfortable truth that often goes unspoken. While tremendous effort is invested in preparing individuals to operate within chaos, far less attention is given to helping them transition back into ordinary life once the mission is over.

When the shift ends, when the deployment ends, when the sirens stop and the uniforms come off, there is often an expectation that the person will simply return to normal. Families, communities, and even the individuals themselves hope that the switch can simply be turned off—that the mindset required for survival in crisis can be neatly packed away until the next call.

But the truth is far more complicated. The mind does not operate like a machine with a simple on-and-off switch. The systems that kept someone alive in dangerous environments—hypervigilance, emotional detachment, rapid threat assessment—do not always disappear when the uniform comes off. In many cases, those systems continue running long after the danger has passed.

The unfortunate reality is that for many of us, the "off switch" was never truly installed in the first place. Or if it was, it stopped working somewhere along the way. The brain learned to stay alert because alertness meant survival. It learned to suppress emotion because emotion could interfere with critical decisions. Those adaptations were necessary in the moment, but they often follow us home whether we want them to or not.

This is where the real struggle begins. The very traits that make someone effective in crisis can make ordinary life feel confusing and overwhelming. A mind trained for chaos may struggle in stillness. A nervous system accustomed to constant adrenaline may feel restless in peaceful environments. Relationships may suffer because the emotional armor that protects us at work does not easily come off when we walk through the front door.

Understanding this process is the first step toward recognizing that the changes we experience are not signs of personal failure. They are often the result of prolonged exposure to environments that require extraordinary levels of resilience and sacrifice.

And that realization leads directly into the next truth—one that many first responders and veterans need to hear but rarely do: sometimes, after everything we have experienced, it is normal not to feel normal anymore.

IT'S NORMAL NOT TO BE NORMAL

The Cost of THE CALL
Finding Healing from PTSD in Christ

The first time I truly realized that I was no longer the same person who had boarded a bus headed for the Military Entrance Processing Station—commonly known as MEPS—I was nineteen years old and returning home from boot camp. Only a few months had passed, but something inside me had shifted in a way I could not fully explain.

Before leaving for training, I was still very much a young man trying to figure out who I was and where I fit in the world. Like many teenagers stepping into adulthood, I carried a mixture of confidence and uncertainty. I had dreams, opinions, and assumptions about life that had never really been tested. I thought I understood myself. I thought I understood the world. Boot camp quickly proved otherwise.

In the span of only a few months, everything about my daily existence changed. The environment, the expectations, the structure, the discipline—every part of the process was designed to reshape the individual. The goal was not simply to train someone physically. The goal was to transform the way you thought, the way you reacted, and the way you understood responsibility and sacrifice.

When I returned home after those first months of training, something inside me felt different. The change was subtle in some ways, yet undeniable in others. I carried myself differently. I thought differently. I reacted to situations with a level of seriousness that had not existed before. Looking back now, I realize that the process of transformation had already begun.

At the time, I could not say whether that change was entirely good or entirely bad. All I knew was that I was not the same person who had left home. In three short months, the young man who boarded that bus had begun to fade, replaced by someone who was learning to operate in a completely different world.

As the years passed, the transformation did not stop there. Each deployment, each operation, and each training exercise added another layer to the process. Experiences accumulated slowly over time, shaping how I viewed people, danger, responsibility, and even life itself. Little by little, pieces of the person I once was seemed to chip away.

This is something many service members and first responders eventually recognize when they look back over their careers. The transformation rarely happens in one dramatic moment. Instead, it happens gradually, almost invisibly, through repeated exposure to intense situations that require a person to think, react, and function differently than most civilians ever will.

Each mission and each crisis leaves its mark. Some experiences strengthen resilience. Others leave emotional scars that take time to understand. But all of them contribute in some way to the evolution of the person standing in the uniform.

Over time, the people closest to us often notice the difference before we do. Family members may say things like, "You've changed," though they may not fully understand why. Loved ones might struggle to reconcile the person they remember with the person who has returned from training, deployment, or years of service.

For the individual going through it, this can be frustrating. Not because the concern is unwelcome, but because the change itself feels necessary. The environments in which soldiers, Marines, police officers, firefighters, and emergency responders operate demand a different mindset. Survival often depends on the ability to adapt quickly, control emotions under pressure, and remain focused in the middle of chaos.

Within the Marine Corps, there is a phrase that captures this concept well: **adapt and overcome**. It is more than a slogan—it is a mindset. The ability to adapt to any environment and overcome any obstacle becomes deeply ingrained in the culture. Recruits are trained to adjust quickly to changing circumstances, push beyond perceived limits, and remain mission-focused no matter how difficult the situation becomes.

But what is often overlooked is that this adaptation is not limited to physical endurance or tactical skill. It affects the mind and the personality as well. The brain begins to rewire itself to prioritize awareness, discipline, and emotional control. Over time, these qualities become second nature.

For those living inside that system, the transformation makes sense. It becomes a necessary part of survival and effectiveness. The problem is that family members and friends who have never experienced those environments often have no framework to understand why the change is happening. From their perspective, it can feel sudden or even alarming.

What they may not realize is that the change is not a rejection of who we were before—it is an adaptation required by the environment we now operate in. In many cases, it is the very process that allows service members and first responders to function effectively in situations that would overwhelm most people.

This same pattern appears throughout the careers of first responders as well. Police officers, firefighters, paramedics, and emergency personnel are exposed to situations that require them to manage chaos, tragedy, and danger on a regular basis. Over time, their mindset begins to shift in order to handle those demands.

The transformation is not optional. It is a natural response to repeated exposure to intense and often traumatic environments. The mind adjusts because it has to. It learns how to filter emotion, prioritize threats, and maintain control in circumstances where panic would only make things worse.

Because of this, many people in these professions begin to feel different from those around them. Conversations that once felt easy may start to feel disconnected. Humor changes. Priorities shift. The ability to relate to everyday concerns sometimes fades because the scale of what has been experienced feels so different.

It is important to understand that this response is not a sign that something is wrong with the person experiencing it. In many ways, it is exactly the opposite. It is evidence that the mind is doing what it was designed to do—adapt to its environment.

In psychology and sociology, the process of reshaping a person's beliefs, behaviors, and social identity within a structured system is often referred to as **resocialization**. This concept describes the unlearning of previous habits and norms and the adoption of new ones that align with the demands of a new environment.

Resocialization commonly occurs in highly structured institutions such as the military, correctional facilities, or specialized training academies. These environments intentionally reshape the way individuals think and behave so that they can function effectively within the system.

In the military, this transformation is reinforced through concepts such as **warrior ethos**, **mental toughness**, and the well-known Marine Corps mindset. These principles are designed to cultivate resilience, discipline, and the ability to endure hardship while remaining focused on the mission. They shape not only what a service member does, but how they see themselves and their role in the world.

Over time, these values become deeply embedded in a person's identity. The uniform may come off at the end of the day, but the mindset remains. The habits of awareness, responsibility, and readiness become part of who the individual is.

This is why so many veterans and first responders struggle when transitioning back into civilian life or attempting to explain their experiences to others. The transformation they have undergone is profound, yet difficult to describe to someone who has never lived through it.

Understanding this reality is essential for both those who serve and the families who support them. Change is not only inevitable—it is part of the process. The environments these men and women operate in require a different version of themselves in order to succeed.

Perhaps the most important truth to recognize is this: after everything they have seen and experienced, it is completely normal for them not to feel normal anymore.

ADAPTING TO CHANGES

The human mind is one of the most remarkable aspects of our existence. The more we study it, the more it reveals a level of complexity that points beyond mere chance. Its ability to process information, adapt to changing circumstances, and guide our decisions is extraordinary. For many believers, the mind itself stands as powerful evidence of a Creator—an intelligent design that equips human beings with the capacity for thought, reflection, choice, and transformation.

One of the most fascinating characteristics of the human mind is its ability to adapt to its environment. Whether a person is placed in a peaceful setting or a chaotic one, the mind begins to adjust almost immediately. It learns patterns, absorbs experiences, and develops responses that allow the individual to function within that environment. In many ways, the mind acts like a sophisticated filter and processor, constantly receiving information and translating it into thoughts, emotions, and actions.

Unlike a machine that simply reacts to programming, the human mind was designed with something even more profound: the ability to exercise free will. While external influences shape our thinking, we are not merely passive recipients of those influences. We have the ability to reflect, evaluate, and choose what we will ultimately believe and how we will respond. This capacity for choice is what gives human life its moral and spiritual dimension.

The mind functions much like a gateway. What we allow to enter through that gateway—what we repeatedly see, hear, and dwell upon—begins to shape our internal world. Over time, those inputs form patterns of thinking that influence how we interpret reality and how we respond to challenges. In other words, the mind processes the information it receives and eventually produces responses that align with that information.

This principle becomes especially important when considering the experiences of first responders, veterans, and anyone regularly exposed to high levels of stress and trauma. The mind absorbs every scene, every conversation, and every intense moment encountered along the way. If those experiences accumulate without any healthy form of renewal or reflection, the mind can begin to operate in a constant state of tension, alertness, or emotional fatigue.

Scripture speaks directly to this reality. In the book of Romans, the apostle Paul writes, "Do not conform to the pattern of this world, but be transformed by the renewing of your mind" (Romans 12:2). This verse carries both a warning and an invitation. The warning is that the world around us constantly pressures us to conform—to think, act, and react according to its patterns. The invitation, however, is that transformation is possible when the mind is renewed.

For those struggling with anxiety, stress, or the lingering effects of trauma, this idea of renewal becomes incredibly important. Renewal does not mean pretending the past never happened. It does not mean ignoring the realities of pain or hardship. Instead, renewal involves gradually replacing destructive patterns of thinking with truth, hope, and perspective that lead toward healing.

When a person begins to engage with God's Word regularly, something remarkable begins to take place. Scripture does more than provide temporary comfort; it reshapes the way we interpret life itself. The promises, wisdom, and guidance found in the Bible begin to challenge the lies that fear and trauma often plant in the mind. Slowly but steadily, the mind learns to anchor itself in truth rather than in the shifting emotions created by difficult experiences.

This transformation rarely happens overnight. Just as unhealthy thinking patterns develop gradually over time, the process of renewal unfolds step by step. Each day spent reflecting on truth, praying, and inviting God into our thoughts adds another layer of strength and clarity to the mind. Over time, the chaos that once dominated our thinking begins to lose its power.

Before many people come to Christ, their minds are often shaped primarily by external influences. The things we watch, listen to, read, and discuss with others all play a role in forming our beliefs and attitudes. Entertainment, social media, cultural expectations, family traditions, and peer influences constantly compete for space within our thoughts.

The challenge is that many of these influences are themselves broken or incomplete. They may offer momentary distraction or emotional stimulation, but they rarely provide lasting truth or guidance. Without realizing it, people can spend years feeding their minds with information that leaves them spiritually and emotionally depleted.

A helpful way to understand this is through a simple comparison. Imagine someone trying to train for a marathon while eating nothing but junk food every day. No matter how much effort they put into their training, their body will eventually struggle because it lacks the proper fuel to perform.

The body requires nourishment that strengthens it rather than weakens it.

The mind works in a very similar way. If we continually feed our minds with negativity, fear, anger, or empty distractions, those influences eventually begin to shape our attitudes and actions. Over time, the results appear in the form of stress, unhealthy habits, destructive thoughts, and a sense of spiritual exhaustion.

For someone who has spent years absorbing these influences, the question naturally arises: how can the mind return to a healthier state? How can someone break free from patterns of thinking that have been reinforced over a long period of time?

The answer begins with a simple but powerful decision—to start today. Regardless of where a person finds themselves mentally or spiritually, change becomes possible the moment they begin feeding their mind with something different. Instead of continuing to consume what drains the soul, they begin to seek out what brings life.

For believers, this life-giving source is found in the Word of God. The Bible describes itself as living and powerful, capable of penetrating deeply into the human heart and mind. Hebrews 4:12 speaks of the Word of God as "sharper than any double-edged sword," able to discern the thoughts and intentions of the heart. This imagery reflects the idea that Scripture reaches into the deepest places of the human soul, exposing what is broken while also pointing toward restoration.

When a person consistently engages with God's Word, the mind begins to realign with truth. Fear is gradually replaced with trust. Confusion begins to give way to clarity. Even the wounds created by years of stress and trauma can begin to heal as the mind learns to rest in something stronger than its own strength.

For many first responders and veterans, the mind has spent years operating in survival mode. Hypervigilance, emotional suppression, and constant readiness may have become second nature. These patterns were necessary in moments of danger, but they can make peace feel unfamiliar when the crisis is over.

This is where spiritual renewal becomes so powerful. By regularly inviting God's truth into our thoughts, we allow the mind to slowly transition from survival mode into a place of restoration. What once felt broken can begin to heal. What once felt overwhelming can gradually become manageable.

The process requires patience and persistence. Healing rarely happens instantly, and there will be days when progress feels slow. Yet every moment spent renewing the mind with truth contributes to a deeper transformation taking place beneath the surface.

Over time, the mind that once felt trapped in chaos can rediscover stability, clarity, and peace. Not because the past has disappeared, but because the mind has learned to process that past through the lens of truth rather than through the weight of fear.

In this way, the same mind that once adapted to survive trauma can also adapt to experience healing. And when guided by God's Word, that renewal becomes not only possible—but powerful enough to restore what once seemed beyond repair.

HEALING TAKES TIME

One of the most difficult truths to accept after experiencing trauma or prolonged stress is this: you will never be exactly the same person you once were. Life has a way of changing us. Experiences shape us, circumstances stretch us, and the moments we walk through—both joyful and painful—leave their mark on who we become.

At first, that realization can feel discouraging. Many people long to go back to the way things were before the hardships, before the loss, before the trauma, or before the weight of responsibility began to accumulate. For first responders and veterans especially, there can be a deep desire to return to the person they were before the uniform, before the deployments, or before the years spent responding to crisis after crisis.

But the reality is that change is a natural part of life. No one remains exactly the same throughout their lifetime. Every person is shaped by the events they encounter, the choices they make, and the lessons they learn along the way. Change is not limited to those who serve in high-stress professions; it happens to every human being.

The difference is that some changes come through ordinary life experiences, while others come through extraordinary challenges. Those who serve as first responders, soldiers, or emergency personnel often experience situations that accelerate this transformation. Exposure to danger, suffering, and responsibility forces the mind and heart to mature in ways that others may never fully understand.

Yet change itself is not inherently bad. In fact, growth often requires change. The real question is not whether we will change, but rather **what direction that change will take**. Will our experiences make us bitter, closed off, and hardened toward life? Or will they lead us toward wisdom, compassion, and a deeper understanding of both ourselves and others?

Every challenge we encounter has the potential to become either a stepping stone or a stumbling block. Some people allow hardship to trap them in anger or despair. Others learn to use those same hardships as opportunities for growth. The difference between those two outcomes often comes down to the choices we make along the way.

Healing, in many ways, is a choice. It is not something that can be forced upon someone from the outside. Friends can encourage it, counselors can guide it, and loved ones can support it—but ultimately, each person must decide for themselves whether they are willing to pursue healing.

This does not mean the journey will be easy. Healing is rarely a quick or simple process. In many cases, it unfolds slowly over months or even years. Emotional wounds, much like physical ones, require time to mend. The deeper the wound, the more patience and care the recovery may require.

For those struggling with trauma, anxiety, or the lingering effects of difficult experiences, it can sometimes feel as though progress is painfully slow. There may be days when it feels like nothing is improving at all. In those moments, it is important to remember that healing is not measured by how quickly it happens, but by the willingness to continue moving forward.

Even small steps in the right direction matter. Each decision to seek truth, to confront pain honestly, and to pursue growth rather than avoidance contributes to the larger process of restoration. The key is not perfection; the key is persistence.

As long as a person continues moving forward rather than retreating into old patterns, progress is still taking place.

The Bible offers many examples of individuals who faced long periods of struggle before experiencing restoration. One particularly powerful story is found in the Gospel of Matthew. In Matthew 9:20–22, we read about a woman who had suffered from a debilitating illness for twelve years. Her condition had consumed much of her life, and despite seeking help from many sources, no one had been able to heal her.

Imagine the level of frustration and hopelessness she must have felt after so many years of searching for relief. Twelve years is a long time to live with pain, uncertainty, and unanswered questions. Yet despite all of her disappointments, she did not give up hope entirely.

At some point, she heard about Jesus and the miracles He was performing. Something within her stirred—a belief that if she could somehow reach Him, her situation could finally change. The Scriptures tell us that she made a bold decision. She said to herself, "If I only touch His garment, I will be healed."

In the cultural context of that time, her condition would have made it socially unacceptable for her to approach a crowd in the way she did. Yet desperation and faith pushed her to act beyond those limitations. She stepped out of what society expected and reached toward something greater.

When she touched the edge of Jesus' garment, the Gospel tells us that she was immediately made whole. Jesus turned and acknowledged her faith, saying, "Take heart, daughter; your faith has made you well." In that moment, years of suffering were brought to an end through a single act of trust.

This story carries a powerful message for anyone seeking healing today. The woman's restoration began long before the physical miracle occurred. It began with a decision in her mind—a decision to believe that change was still possible despite everything she had experienced.

In much the same way, emotional and spiritual healing often begins internally before it becomes visible externally. A person must first decide that they are willing to pursue healing. That decision opens the door for change to begin.

For those dealing with the emotional wounds of trauma, the process may take time. Healing rarely unfolds in a single moment. Yet every step toward truth, every moment spent renewing the mind with God's Word, and every act of faith contributes to the gradual restoration of the soul.

The renewal of the mind plays a crucial role in this journey. When a person consistently fills their thoughts with truth, hope, and spiritual guidance, the mind slowly begins to release the patterns of fear and despair that trauma can create. Over time, what once felt overwhelming begins to lose its grip.

This does not mean that difficult days will disappear completely. Even the strongest men and women of faith experienced moments of discouragement and struggle. The Bible is filled with stories of people who wrestled with fear, doubt, exhaustion, and hardship.

These stories were not included in Scripture by accident. They serve as reminders that no human being is perfect. Every person—even those chosen for great purposes—walks through seasons of weakness and difficulty.

The encouraging truth is that God does not expect perfection from us. Perfection belongs to Christ alone. What God desires is a heart that continues to seek Him, even in the middle of the struggle.

As believers pursue that relationship, Scripture teaches that God continues shaping and refining them throughout their lives. The apostle Paul described this process as being transformed "from glory to glory," meaning that spiritual growth happens gradually as we walk with God over time.

For someone seeking healing, this perspective can bring great comfort. The journey does not have to be completed all at once. It unfolds day by day, step by step, as God works within us to restore what has been broken.

So if you find yourself on a long road toward healing, do not lose heart. Progress may be slow, but slow progress is still progress. Each day that you choose to move forward, no matter how small the step may seem, is a victory.

Healing takes time—but with faith, persistence, and the renewing power of God's truth, it is a journey that can lead not only to recovery, but to a deeper and stronger version of the person you are becoming.

WAITING IN THE HALLWAY

There is a familiar saying that many people repeat during seasons of change: *when one door closes, another door opens.* The phrase is meant to bring comfort, reminding us that endings are often followed by new beginnings. Yet there is a part of that process that is rarely discussed—the time spent in between.

What happens in the hallway between those doors?

When one chapter of life ends and the next has not yet begun, we often find ourselves standing in a place of uncertainty. The door behind us has closed, and the door ahead of us has not yet opened. This in-between space can feel uncomfortable, confusing, and even discouraging.

For many people—especially those recovering from trauma, loss, or major life transitions—this hallway can feel like the longest stretch of the journey. Healing takes time, and during that time it may seem as though life has slowed down while everyone else continues moving forward.

In those moments, difficult questions often begin to surface. Should we feel sorry for ourselves? Should we withdraw from others and hide from the world until things somehow improve? Should we simply give up and accept that life will never change?

These thoughts are more common than many people are willing to admit. Almost everyone who walks through a season of pain or uncertainty has moments when they feel like retreating from the world. The temptation to isolate ourselves can become strong, especially when we feel misunderstood or exhausted by the effort it takes to keep going.

Isolation, however, rarely brings the healing we hope it will. While withdrawing from others may seem like a form of protection, it often deepens the sense of loneliness and discouragement that we are already carrying. What begins as a temporary retreat can gradually become a place where hope begins to fade.

So what should we do while we are waiting in the hallway?

One of the most powerful yet overlooked tools available to us during these seasons is the act of sharing our story. Opening up about our thoughts, struggles, and progress is rarely easy.

Many people, particularly first responders and veterans, have been conditioned to handle difficulties privately. Strength is often associated with silence, and vulnerability can feel uncomfortable or even risky.

Yet there is something deeply powerful about sharing our experiences with others. When we speak honestly about what we have walked through, two important things begin to happen. First, we remind ourselves that we are not alone in our struggles. Second, we create an opportunity for others to find encouragement through our journey.

Stories have always held tremendous power. Throughout history, personal testimonies have inspired courage, strengthened faith, and helped others see that healing and transformation are possible. In many ways, our experiences become bridges that connect us with others who are walking through similar challenges.

The Bible speaks about this idea in the book of Revelation. In describing those who overcame great adversity, Scripture says that they triumphed "by the blood of the Lamb and by the word of their testimony" (Revelation 12:11). In other words, their victory was not only rooted in God's power but also in their willingness to declare what God had done in their lives.

A testimony is more than just a story—it is evidence of God's faithfulness in the midst of difficulty. It reminds us of where we have been and how far we have come. It points to the ways God has carried us through situations that once seemed impossible to survive.

Unfortunately, many people underestimate the power of their testimony. They may believe that their experiences are too ordinary or too painful to share. Others may assume that their struggles disqualify them from encouraging someone else. In reality, it is often those very struggles that make a testimony meaningful and relatable.

One of the clearest biblical examples of this principle can be found in the story of David. Before David ever faced the giant Goliath, he had already encountered smaller but equally dangerous battles while tending his father's sheep. On separate occasions, he fought off both a lion and a bear that had threatened his flock.

When David later stood before King Saul and volunteered to confront Goliath, Saul initially doubted his ability. David was young and inexperienced in comparison to the battle-hardened warrior standing across the valley. Yet David responded by sharing his testimony. He reminded Saul that God had already delivered him from the lion and the bear, and he expressed confidence that the same God would help him defeat the giant.

David's confidence did not come from pride in his own abilities. It came from remembering what God had already done. His past experiences had built a foundation of faith that he could rely on in the face of an even greater challenge.

This same principle applies to many of the men and women reading these words. If you have served in the military, worked as a first responder, or faced significant personal trials, chances are you have already overcome situations that others might not have survived. The strength and resilience you demonstrated during those moments are not meaningless—they are part of your testimony.

Even if you feel like you are still in the middle of the struggle, the fact that you are still standing is itself a powerful statement. Your story carries weight because it reflects endurance, courage, and the ability to keep moving forward even when circumstances were overwhelming.

Sharing that story can help others in ways you may never fully see. Someone who feels alone in their pain may hear your experience and realize that they are not the only one fighting that battle. Someone who feels ready to give up may discover new strength simply by hearing how you continued moving forward despite your own difficulties.

At the same time, speaking about your journey can also play a significant role in your own healing. Expressing thoughts and emotions that have been carried silently for years can release a weight that many people did not realize they were holding. What once felt like a private burden becomes part of a larger story of growth and restoration.

The apostle Paul offered encouragement for those who feel weary along the way. In Galatians 6:9, he writes, "Let us not grow weary of doing good, for in due season we will reap, if we do not give up." This verse serves as a reminder that perseverance often precedes breakthrough. The harvest may not appear immediately, but the promise remains for those who continue moving forward.

Waiting in the hallway does not mean that nothing is happening. Even when progress feels slow, important work is taking place beneath the surface. Growth, healing, and preparation often occur during the quiet seasons when it seems like life is standing still.

Instead of viewing the hallway as wasted time, it can be helpful to see it as a place of preparation. It is an opportunity to reflect on what God has already done, to strengthen your faith, and to encourage others who may be walking through similar challenges.

Your story matters. Your experiences matter. And the lessons you have learned along the way can become a source of strength not only for you but for many others who are searching for hope.

So while you wait in the hallway, do not lose heart. Continue growing, continue trusting, and continue sharing what God has done in your life. The door ahead may not have opened yet, but the journey through the hallway is already shaping the person you are becoming.

Chapter Three Reflection - *The Change*

Change is one of the few guarantees in life. For first responders, veterans, and anyone who has spent years walking into situations most people run away from, that change can feel especially dramatic. The experiences we face reshape the way we see the world, the way we react to danger, and even the way we relate to the people closest to us. Sometimes we do not even realize how much we have changed until someone points it out—or until we catch a glimpse of ourselves and realize we are no longer the same person we once were.

At first, that realization can be unsettling. Many people long for the version of themselves that existed before the trauma, before the deployments, before the endless calls for service. But the truth is that life is constantly shaping us. The question is not whether change will happen—it always does. The real question is whether that change will lead us toward healing and growth or toward isolation and despair.

For those who have spent years adapting to chaos, it is important to understand that the mind was designed to adjust to its environment. The emotional armor, heightened awareness, and survival mindset developed in high-stress professions are not signs of weakness. They are signs that the mind was doing exactly what it was designed to do—protect you in situations that demanded strength and control.

Recognizing this truth allows us to release the shame that many people carry. Feeling different after years of trauma exposure is not abnormal—it is a natural response to extraordinary circumstances. In many ways, it is normal not to feel normal after everything you have seen and experienced.

Yet Chapter Three also reminds us that while the mind adapts to survive trauma, it can also be renewed for healing. Scripture teaches that transformation begins with the renewing of the mind. What we feed our thoughts will eventually shape our perspective, our emotions, and our actions. When the mind is filled with fear and chaos, the heart struggles to find peace. But when the mind is renewed with truth, hope, and faith, healing slowly begins to take root.

This process takes time. Healing rarely happens overnight. Just as trauma develops over years of exposure, restoration often unfolds gradually as we choose—day after day—to move forward rather than backward. There will be good days and difficult days, moments of clarity and moments of frustration. But progress is not measured by perfection; it is measured by persistence.

Even the seasons of waiting, the moments when it feels like nothing is changing, can hold purpose. Those hallway moments between closed doors and new opportunities are often where God does some of His deepest work in our lives. During those times, our testimony becomes a powerful tool—not only for helping others but also for reminding ourselves of the faithfulness of God throughout the journey.

Chapter Three ultimately reminds us that change does not have to be the end of who we once were. Instead, it can become the beginning of who God is shaping us to become. The same resilience that helped us survive the chaos can now guide us toward healing, growth, and a deeper understanding of God's presence in our lives.

A Small Prayer

Lord,

You know every experience that has shaped my life—the victories, the wounds, and the moments that changed me forever. Sometimes I struggle to understand the person I have become, and at times I miss the version of myself that existed before the pain.

Help me to trust that You are still working in my life, even in the middle of the changes I do not fully understand. Renew my mind with Your truth and give me the strength to keep moving forward, even when the healing process feels slow.

Teach me to use my experiences not as a source of shame, but as a testimony of Your faithfulness. Help me encourage others who may be walking through similar struggles.

Remind me that I am not alone, that You are with me in every step of this journey, and that the work You have started in my life will not be left unfinished.

Amen.

Practical Takeaway - *Practice daily renewal of the mind.*

Healing often begins with what we allow to occupy our thoughts. Take a few minutes each day to intentionally shift your focus away from the stress and chaos that may dominate your mind.

Try the following simple practice:

1. **Start the day with truth.** Read a short passage of Scripture or a devotional that reminds you of God's promises.

2. **Reflect honestly.** Take a moment to acknowledge how you are truly feeling—without judgment or shame.

3. **Speak life over your thoughts.** Remind yourself that change is part of the journey and that healing takes time.

4. **Share part of your story.** Talk with a trusted friend, mentor, or fellow first responder about your experiences. Honest conversation can be one of the most powerful tools for healing.

You do not have to solve everything today. The goal is simply to keep moving forward—one step, one day, and one renewed thought at a time.

THE BATTLE WITHIN

"Fight the good fight of the faith. Take hold of the eternal life to which you were called when you made your good confession in the presence of many witnesses."

I TIMOTHY 6:12

For many people who live with trauma, every day can feel like a quiet struggle. Some days are manageable, while others feel overwhelming, but beneath the surface there is often a constant tension taking place within the mind and heart. For those dealing with Post-Traumatic Stress Disorder, this internal conflict can become one of the most exhausting parts of the healing journey.

PTSD does not simply affect memories of past events; it creates an ongoing struggle between the desire to feel safe and the persistent reminders of experiences that once threatened that safety. Even when a person is no longer in danger, the mind can remain trapped in a heightened state of alertness. The brain, having learned to protect itself during traumatic moments, continues to react as if the threat could return at any moment.

As a result, the world may begin to feel unpredictable and unsafe, even in environments that should feel peaceful. A crowded room, a loud noise, or even an unfamiliar place can trigger an internal alarm that the person cannot easily turn off. This constant sense of vigilance places the nervous system in a prolonged state of survival mode.

Living in that state for long periods of time affects more than just the individual—it also impacts the people closest to them. Relationships often become strained as loved ones struggle to understand what is happening internally. Friends may interpret withdrawal as disinterest. Spouses may feel shut out of emotional conversations. Social interactions that once felt natural can begin to feel exhausting or even threatening.

This is where the battle within becomes most visible. The person who wants healing may find themselves fighting against their own instincts. The very actions that could help restore connection and peace—talking openly, seeking support, allowing others to help—can feel incredibly difficult to take.

Instead of reaching out, the natural response often becomes withdrawal. Instead of sharing thoughts and emotions, silence feels safer. Instead of stepping into community, isolation begins to look like protection. The mind convinces itself that remaining alone will prevent further pain.

Unfortunately, isolation rarely provides the relief it promises. While it may feel like a temporary shield, it often deepens the darkness that trauma creates. Conversations that could bring understanding never happen. Support that could bring strength is never received. Over time, the silence can make a person feel even more trapped within their own thoughts.

Many first responders and veterans genuinely desire to get better. They do not want to live with the weight of trauma or the limitations that sometimes come with it. In fact, many of them remember a time when life felt much different.

There was a time when they could move freely without constantly scanning their surroundings. There was a time when traveling to new places felt exciting rather than stressful. There was a time when their minds were not filled with intrusive thoughts or sudden flashes of memories that refused to fade away.

Remembering that earlier version of themselves can sometimes create another layer of pain. It can make a person question their strength or wonder what happened to the confidence they once carried. Some may even begin to feel ashamed, as though the presence of fear or anxiety somehow reflects a lack of courage.

Those feelings can be particularly difficult for individuals who spent years working in professions built around bravery and control. First responders and veterans are trained to face danger directly, to remain calm in chaotic situations, and to protect others even when their own safety is at risk. When trauma begins to affect their internal world, it can feel like a betrayal of the identity they once held.

Yet the truth is that trauma does not erase courage. The fact that someone continues to face each day despite the internal struggle is itself a form of bravery. The battle may no longer be taking place on a battlefield or in the middle of an emergency call, but it is still a battle nonetheless.

What many people rarely discuss is how much trauma can quietly steal from a person's life. Opportunities may be avoided because unfamiliar environments trigger anxiety. Relationships may fade because emotional distance feels safer than vulnerability. Experiences that once brought joy may be replaced by hesitation and fear.

These losses often occur gradually, making them difficult to recognize until years have passed. The person may still be functioning in daily life—working, providing, and fulfilling responsibilities—but internally they may feel as though pieces of their life have been slowly taken away.

The struggle between who they once were and who they feel they have become creates a powerful inner conflict. It is the desire to live freely again battling against the protective mechanisms the mind developed to survive trauma.

Interestingly, the Bible speaks openly about this kind of internal struggle. Even the apostle Paul, one of the most influential leaders of the early Christian church, described experiencing a battle within himself. Paul endured immense hardship throughout his life. He faced persecution, imprisonment, physical suffering, and constant threats to his safety. If anyone understood what it meant to carry emotional and spiritual burdens, it was Paul.

In his letter to the Romans, Paul described a struggle that many people can relate to. In Romans 7:15–20, he spoke about wanting to do what was right but finding himself doing the very things he wished to avoid. He expressed frustration with the conflict between his intentions and his actions, describing it as a battle taking place within his own heart.

Paul's honesty in these verses is incredibly important. It reminds us that internal conflict is not a sign that something is fundamentally wrong with us. Even individuals of great faith and strength experience moments when their thoughts, emotions, and actions feel out of alignment.

But Paul did not end his reflection in despair. After describing the struggle, he pointed to the source of hope that sustained him. In Romans 7:25, he declared that the answer to this internal battle ultimately comes through Jesus Christ.

For Paul, healing did not come from relying solely on his own strength or discipline. Instead, it came from recognizing that God's grace was greater than the conflict he experienced within himself. Christ offered not only forgiveness but also transformation—a path toward freedom that did not depend entirely on human effort.

This truth carries powerful meaning for anyone struggling with the inner battle created by trauma. Healing does not require us to fight alone. The same God who offers salvation also offers restoration for the wounded parts of our lives.

Surrendering our struggles to Christ does not mean that the battle disappears instantly. Healing, as we have already seen, often unfolds gradually. But surrender allows us to place the weight of that struggle into hands far stronger than our own.

Each day becomes an opportunity to release a little more of

that burden. Each moment spent trusting God allows His presence to work within our hearts and minds. Over time, the transformation that once seemed impossible begins to take shape.

The intrusive thoughts may still appear from time to time. Memories may still surface unexpectedly. Yet something important begins to change: we no longer face those moments alone.

Through the presence of the Holy Spirit, believers are given a helper, a guide, and a source of strength that remains with them even in their darkest moments. Instead of relying only on our own ability to fight the battle, we learn to trust the One who fights alongside us.

The battle within may still exist, but it is no longer hopeless. With Christ walking beside us, even the deepest struggles can become part of a journey toward healing, restoration, and a renewed sense of purpose.

THE FIGHT MATTERS

Continuing the fight can be exhausting. Many first responders and veterans are no strangers to battles fought on the outside. They understand what it means to face danger, to identify a threat, and to push forward despite fear or fatigue. In an external battle, the enemy is visible. The objective is clear. The mission is defined. Even when the situation is dangerous, there is a certain clarity about what must be done.

The internal battle, however, is very different. The enemy is not always visible, and the battlefield exists within the mind and heart. Thoughts, emotions, memories, and fears can rise unexpectedly, creating a struggle that is far more difficult to define. There are no clear front lines and no obvious moment when the conflict ends. For many people living with trauma, the internal fight can feel far more exhausting than any physical confrontation they have ever faced.

In these moments it can be tempting to give up the fight entirely. When exhaustion sets in, the mind may begin to question whether the effort is worth it. Some may wonder if it would be easier to simply withdraw, to stop trying to overcome the internal struggles that seem to return again and again.

Yet the truth is that the fight itself matters. Choosing to keep moving forward, even in the face of internal exhaustion, is one of the most powerful acts of courage a person can demonstrate. The decision to continue seeking healing, connection, and purpose is not a small one. It is a declaration that the pain will not have the final word.

One of the greatest examples of perseverance in the face of suffering can be found in the life of Jesus Christ. When God entered the world in human form, He did not do so without understanding the cost. Jesus knew from the beginning what His mission would require. He knew the rejection, the suffering, and ultimately the sacrifice that awaited Him on the cross.

Despite this knowledge, Jesus chose to continue forward. He did not turn away from the path set before Him, even when that path led to immense physical and emotional pain. The question that naturally arises is this: what gave Him the strength to endure such suffering?

The answer is found in Hebrews 12:2, which explains that Jesus endured the cross "for the joy that was set before Him." In other words, His focus was not solely on the suffering He would experience in the present moment. Instead, He looked beyond the pain and saw the purpose that lay on the other side of the cross.

Jesus understood that His sacrifice would open the door for redemption and restoration for countless people. Because of His willingness to endure suffering, humanity would have the opportunity to be reconciled with God. The joy of that future reality gave Him the strength to persevere through the darkest moment of His earthly life.

This perspective carries a powerful lesson for anyone engaged in their own internal battles. When we focus only on the pain of the present moment, the struggle can feel overwhelming. But when we remember the purpose that lies beyond the struggle—the possibility of healing, restored relationships, and renewed life—the fight begins to take on deeper meaning.

Scripture reminds us that love is often the driving force behind perseverance. In John 15:13, Jesus declares that there is no greater love than to lay down one's life for one's friends. While most people may never be called to make a sacrifice as great as Christ's, the principle remains the same: love gives us the strength to endure what would otherwise feel impossible.

For many veterans and first responders, love is one of the primary reasons they continue fighting their internal battles. They fight because of the love they have for their families. They fight because they want to be present for their children, their spouses, and the people who depend on them. They fight because they believe that their lives still hold meaning and purpose.

This idea is illustrated beautifully in the story of Nehemiah in the Old Testament. After the nation of Israel had been exiled to Babylon, many of the Jewish people eventually returned to Jerusalem. What they discovered, however, was heartbreaking. The walls surrounding the city had been destroyed, leaving the entire community vulnerable to attack from their enemies.

In ancient times, city walls were essential for protection. Without them, the people of Jerusalem were exposed and defenseless. The broken walls were not only a physical problem but also a symbol of the nation's vulnerability and brokenness.

Nehemiah, who served as the cupbearer to the king of Babylon, learned about the condition of Jerusalem and was deeply moved. Although he held a comfortable and influential position within the king's court, he could not ignore the suffering of his people. His heart was burdened by the knowledge that the city of his ancestors lay unprotected and vulnerable.

Through prayer and faith, Nehemiah sought God's guidance. In time, God granted him favor with the king, who allowed him to travel to Jerusalem and lead the effort to rebuild the city's walls. Nehemiah gathered the people together, and they began the difficult work of restoring the defenses of their city.

As the rebuilding progressed, opposition quickly arose. Several enemies of Israel—Sanballat, Geshem, and Tobiah—began mocking and threatening the workers. They attempted to discourage the people and intimidate them into abandoning the project.

Despite these threats, Nehemiah refused to allow fear to stop the work. In Nehemiah 4:14, he addressed the people and reminded them of the reason they were fighting. He encouraged them with these words: "Remember the Lord, who is great and awesome, and fight for your brothers, your sons, your daughters, your wives, and your homes."

Nehemiah understood that when people remember what they are fighting for, they find strength they did not realize they possessed. The men and women rebuilding the wall were not simply performing construction work. They were protecting their families, their future, and their faith.

In many ways, the internal battles faced by those living with trauma resemble that moment in Nehemiah's story. There are voices that attempt to discourage us—voices of fear, doubt, and exhaustion. There are moments when it feels easier to stop building and walk away from the work of healing.

But just like the people of Jerusalem, we must remember why the fight matters. We fight because our lives matter. We fight because the people we love matter. We fight because future generations can benefit from the strength and perseverance we demonstrate today.

Healing may not happen quickly, and the battle may feel long at times. Yet every step forward, no matter how small, is meaningful. Progress does not require perfection. It simply requires persistence.

Sometimes the fight will be measured in days. Other times it will be measured in hours or even minutes. On difficult days, victory may simply mean choosing not to give up.

The important thing is to remain in the fight. Step by step, moment by moment, healing continues to move forward. And as long as we keep going, the battle within does not define our ending—it becomes part of the story of our perseverance.

YOU ARE NOT ALONE

One of the most painful aspects of living with trauma is the overwhelming feeling of loneliness that can settle deep within the heart. For many individuals struggling with Post-Traumatic Stress Disorder, the sense of isolation can be just as difficult as the memories themselves. It is a strange and unsettling experience—to be surrounded by people and yet feel completely alone.

As a first responder, I came to know that feeling all too well. There were moments when I could stand in a room full of people—friends, family, or coworkers—and still feel like the loneliest person present. Conversations continued around me, laughter filled the air, and yet internally it felt as though I was standing on the outside of it all, unable to fully connect with what was happening.

Part of this feeling comes from the belief that no one around you can truly understand what you have experienced. The events that first responders and veterans witness often exist outside the normal experiences of everyday life. When you have seen the worst moments of humanity—violence, tragedy, loss, and suffering—it can be difficult to imagine that anyone else could truly relate to what lives inside your mind.

At other times, the loneliness is not caused by the absence of understanding but by the depth of the emotional struggle itself. Trauma can pull a person inward, creating a kind of emotional cave where thoughts and memories echo in isolation. Even when others are present and willing to listen, the mind can convince itself that staying silent is safer than speaking honestly about the pain.

Living this way is emotionally exhausting. Maintaining the appearance that everything is fine requires tremendous effort. Smiling when you feel broken inside, engaging in conversations when your mind is elsewhere, and pretending that the weight you carry does not exist can slowly drain a person's energy. Over time, the pressure of holding everything inside can become overwhelming.

Many people who experience this kind of loneliness begin to withdraw further. Social gatherings may start to feel uncomfortable or even threatening. The effort required to appear "normal" becomes so tiring that isolation begins to feel like the easier option. Unfortunately, the more a person withdraws, the deeper the feeling of loneliness can grow.

Interestingly, this sense of isolation is not unique to modern struggles. Throughout history, even individuals of great faith and courage have experienced moments when they believed they were completely alone. One powerful example is found in the story of the prophet Elijah in the Old Testament.

In 1 Kings 19, Elijah had just experienced one of the most dramatic moments of his ministry. On Mount Carmel, he confronted the prophets of Baal and witnessed God demonstrate His power in a miraculous way. Fire came down from heaven and consumed the offering, proving that the Lord alone was the true God. It was a moment of incredible spiritual victory.

Yet shortly after this event, Elijah's circumstances changed dramatically. Queen Jezebel, furious about the defeat of the prophets of Baal, sent a message threatening Elijah's life. Suddenly, the same man who had stood boldly before hundreds of false prophets found himself running for his life.

Fear and exhaustion overtook him. Elijah fled into the wilderness and eventually found refuge in a cave, where he spent the night in deep distress. When God spoke to him, Elijah poured out his frustration and despair. He told the Lord that he had faithfully served Him, yet now his life was in danger. In his discouragement, Elijah declared that he was the only prophet of the Lord left.

From Elijah's perspective, he truly believed he was completely alone. The pressure, fear, and exhaustion had clouded his view of reality. What he did not realize was that God had already preserved many others who remained faithful. Elijah's feeling of isolation, though very real to him, was not the full truth of the situation.

God responded to Elijah not with condemnation, but with compassion and guidance. First, He demonstrated His power through dramatic displays of nature—a powerful wind, an earthquake, and a fire. Yet the Scriptures tell us that the voice of God was not found in those overwhelming displays. Instead, God spoke to Elijah through what the Bible describes as a "gentle whisper."

That quiet moment carried a profound lesson. In a world often filled with chaos, noise, and constant pressure, the voice of God is frequently heard in the stillness rather than the storm.

Elijah's renewal began not with dramatic action but with a quiet encounter with God's presence.

During that encounter, God reminded Elijah that he was not alone. In fact, there were thousands in Israel who had not turned away from the Lord. Elijah's perspective had been limited by his pain and fear, but God revealed a much larger reality.

God also reminded Elijah that his work was not finished. He gave him new instructions and a renewed mission, including the task of anointing Elisha as his successor. In other words, Elijah's story was far from over. Even in his moment of despair, God still had a purpose for his life.

This story offers a powerful reminder for anyone who feels isolated by trauma or emotional pain. Feelings of loneliness can be incredibly convincing, but they do not always reflect the full truth of our situation. Even when we feel completely alone, we are often surrounded by people who care deeply for us—family members, friends, counselors, mentors, and fellow believers who are willing to walk beside us.

More importantly, we are never alone in a spiritual sense. God's presence does not disappear during our moments of weakness or struggle. In fact, those moments are often when His presence becomes most meaningful.

When we spend time in prayer and immerse ourselves in God's Word, we begin to rediscover that quiet voice that spoke to Elijah in the cave. In those moments of stillness, God gently reminds us that our lives still have meaning and purpose.

He reminds us that the people around us care more than we may realize. He reminds us that healing is possible, even if the journey takes time. And perhaps most importantly, He reminds us that our story is not finished.

No matter how dark the moment may feel, God continues to work in ways we cannot always see. He places people in our lives who are willing to support us, guide us, and stand beside us during the difficult seasons.

Just as Elijah discovered in that quiet cave, the feeling of being alone does not mean that we truly are. God remains present, our purpose remains intact, and the journey forward is still unfolding.

THE MISSION IS NOT OVER

In his moment of deep discouragement, the prophet Elijah believed that his life and ministry had come to an end. Exhausted, fearful, and overwhelmed by the threats against him, he retreated into isolation and convinced himself that everything he had done for God had been in vain. From his perspective, the mission was over. The victories he had once experienced seemed distant, and the purpose that once drove him forward now felt empty.

Many first responders and veterans experience a similar feeling at some point in their lives. For years they operate in environments where purpose is clear and immediate. The mission is defined. The responsibilities are unmistakable. Each day brings challenges that require courage, discipline, and commitment. In those moments, life often feels meaningful because the work directly impacts the safety and well-being of others.

But eventually, the season of service comes to an end. Sometimes that transition happens because a military commitment has been fulfilled. Other times it occurs through retirement, injury, or circumstances beyond one's control. Regardless of how it happens, the day eventually arrives when the uniform comes off for the last time.

For many, that moment can feel far more difficult than expected. While others may celebrate the transition into civilian life, the individual leaving service may experience a deep sense of uncertainty. The structure that once guided daily life disappears. The camaraderie shared with fellow service members or colleagues fades as everyone moves in different directions. The constant sense of mission that once defined every decision suddenly feels absent.

The Cost of THE CALL

Finding Healing from PTSD in Christ

During active service, many people thrive in the very environments that others find overwhelming. The chaos, the urgency, and the responsibility create a sense of clarity. When lives are on the line, decisions matter. Actions have immediate consequences. There is little room for hesitation, and every member of the team understands the importance of their role.

In those environments, individuals often discover a deep sense of belonging. They feel part of something greater than themselves. They know their efforts contribute to a larger purpose, and that purpose provides motivation even during the most difficult moments.

When that season ends, however, the transition can leave a person feeling disoriented. The tools that once defined their identity—the badge, the uniform, the rifle, the radio, or the gear—are no longer part of their daily life. What once symbolized responsibility and purpose is suddenly absent.

For some, this shift can trigger feelings of anxiety, loneliness, and even betrayal. The world they once knew so well continues moving forward without them. The mission they dedicated themselves to now belongs to someone else. In those quiet moments, many begin to question where they belong and whether their life still holds the same significance it once did.

These emotions mirror the despair Elijah experienced when he sat alone in that cave. After witnessing God perform incredible miracles through his ministry, Elijah suddenly felt abandoned and defeated. The same prophet who had boldly stood before kings and false prophets now believed he had nothing left to offer.

Yet God saw Elijah's situation very differently. While Elijah believed his story had ended, God knew that Elijah's work was not finished. Rather than allowing him to remain in isolation, God gently redirected him toward a new purpose.

God instructed Elijah to return to the wilderness and continue his work. Part of that work involved anointing a new leader—Elisha—who would eventually carry the prophetic ministry forward. In essence, Elijah's next assignment was not to perform dramatic miracles or confront kings, but to mentor and prepare the next generation.

This shift may not have been what Elijah expected. After years of being the central figure in God's prophetic work, he was now being called to invest his wisdom and experience into someone else. Yet this new mission was just as important as the previous one. By mentoring Elisha, Elijah ensured that the work God had begun would continue long after his own life.

The same principle often applies to those transitioning from careers in military service or emergency response. The end of one mission does not mean that purpose has disappeared. Instead, it often signals the beginning of a different kind of mission—one that uses the wisdom gained from past experiences to impact others in new ways.

Everything a person has endured, learned, and overcome throughout their years of service carries value. The resilience developed in difficult situations, the discipline forged through adversity, and the compassion formed through witnessing human suffering are not experiences that simply disappear when the uniform is removed.

God does not waste the experiences of our past. Even the painful moments, the failures, and the struggles can become tools that help guide and encourage others who are walking through similar challenges.

A verse that is often quoted in this context is Romans 8:28. Many people are familiar with the statement that "all things work together for good for those who love God, who are called according to His purpose." Unfortunately, this verse is sometimes misunderstood. Some interpret it to mean that every event in life will immediately result in something positive or beneficial.

In reality, the verse points to something deeper. It reminds believers that God can take every experience—both good and painful—and weave them together in a way that ultimately fulfills His greater purpose. This does not mean that suffering itself is good, nor does it minimize the real pain people experience. Instead, it means that God has the ability to bring meaning and redemption even out of the most difficult circumstances.

The life of the apostle Paul provides a powerful example of this truth. Paul endured tremendous hardship during his ministry. He faced imprisonment, persecution, physical suffering, and constant danger. From a human perspective, many of these events might appear tragic or unjust.

Yet through Paul's faithfulness and obedience, the message of the Gospel spread throughout the ancient world. His letters, written during some of his most difficult moments, continue to inspire and guide millions of people today. What once appeared to be suffering without purpose ultimately became a testimony that continues to glorify God.

For first responders and veterans, this truth can offer profound hope. The challenges, trauma, and sacrifices experienced during years of service do not have to be meaningless. When placed in God's hands, those experiences can become part of a much larger story—one that brings encouragement, wisdom, and healing to others.

The mission may look different than it once did, but it is far from over. Instead of responding to emergencies or serving on the front lines, the new mission may involve mentoring others, sharing personal experiences, supporting fellow veterans or first responders, or guiding people who are struggling with the same battles that were once fought alone.

Purpose does not disappear when a career ends. In many ways, it simply evolves into something deeper and more lasting. The lessons learned through hardship become the very tools that allow us to serve others in ways we never imagined before.

Just as God reminded Elijah that his story was not finished, He continues to remind us that our lives still carry meaning. There are still people who can benefit from our experiences, our wisdom, and our testimony.

The uniform may no longer be part of our daily lives, but the character forged during those years remains. The courage, discipline, and perseverance developed through service are qualities that can continue to impact the world long after the original mission has ended.

In God's plan, no experience is wasted. Even the most painful chapters of our lives can become the foundation for something greater. When we allow Him to guide the next step of our journey, our past can become a powerful instrument that blesses others and brings glory to Him.

THE CAVE EXPERIENCE

There are seasons in life when it feels as though progress has come to a halt. You may feel as though you are stuck in the same place, spinning your wheels without moving forward. Every attempt to change your circumstances seems to lead back to the same point of frustration. During those moments it is easy to believe that something has gone terribly wrong. Yet, what often feels like stagnation may actually be a necessary part of the process God is using to shape our lives.

Throughout Scripture, we find examples of individuals who experienced similar seasons—times when their lives seemed to move in the opposite direction of what they expected. One of the most powerful examples is found in the life of David during his time in the Cave of Adullam. What appeared to be a period of retreat and defeat ultimately became a place of preparation for the future God had already planned for him.

David's story leading up to the cave is remarkable. As a young shepherd, he had already experienced the favor of God in extraordinary ways. He was chosen and anointed by the prophet Samuel to become the future king of Israel, even while the current king, Saul, still ruled. David also achieved national recognition after defeating the giant Goliath, an act that made him a hero in the eyes of the people.

From a human perspective, it would seem logical that

David's path would lead directly to the palace. After all, he had been anointed by God and had already proven his courage and faith. Yet instead of stepping immediately into his destiny as king, David's life took a dramatic and painful turn.

King Saul, once David's mentor and leader, became consumed by jealousy. Rather than celebrating David's victories, Saul began to view him as a threat. That jealousy eventually grew into hatred, and Saul made several attempts on David's life. The man who had once served faithfully in Saul's court suddenly found himself fleeing for survival.

According to 1 Samuel 22:1–2, David escaped and sought refuge in the Cave of Adullam. What had once been a rising life of honor and opportunity was now reduced to hiding in a dark cave while the king of Israel pursued him. It must have been an incredibly confusing and painful moment in David's life.

Imagine the questions that must have filled his mind. David had been faithful to God. He had obeyed the calling placed upon his life. Yet instead of sitting in the palace preparing to rule, he was hiding in isolation. The promises spoken over his life seemed far away, almost impossible to reconcile with his present reality.

Feelings of betrayal likely weighed heavily on him as well. Saul had once been someone David respected deeply—a leader, a mentor, and a man chosen by God to lead the nation. Now that same man was actively seeking his death. For David, the cave represented more than physical shelter; it became a place where he wrestled with the emotional pain of rejection, confusion, and disappointment.

Many people who have experienced trauma or major life transitions can relate to this type of season. There are moments when we feel as though our lives have been pushed into a cave—away from the purpose we once believed we were moving toward. We may find ourselves asking the same questions David likely asked: *What did I do wrong? Why is this happening? Where is God in the middle of this situation?*

Yet what David did not fully understand at the time was that the cave was not a place of abandonment. It was a place of preparation. Before David could rule as king, God was shaping his character in ways that could only occur through hardship and humility.

Scripture consistently teaches that God's definition of greatness is different from the world's definition. In Matthew 23:12, Jesus explains that those who exalt themselves will be humbled, and those who humble themselves will be exalted. True leadership in God's kingdom is not built on status or recognition; it is built on humility, obedience, and trust.

The cave became the environment where those qualities

were developed in David's life. While David may have felt that everything was falling apart, God was quietly shaping him into the kind of leader Israel would need. The cave stripped away the comfort of royal courts and forced David to rely completely on God's guidance and provision.

During this time, David poured out his emotions to God with remarkable honesty. One example of this can be found in Psalm 13, where David expresses the deep frustration and sorrow he felt during his suffering. In Psalm 13:1–2, he cries out, "How long, Lord? Will you forget me forever? How long will you hide your face from me? How long must I wrestle with my thoughts and day after day have sorrow in my heart?"

These words reveal the depth of David's emotional struggle. He was not pretending that everything was fine. He was honest about his pain, his confusion, and his longing for relief. Yet this honesty was not a sign of weak faith—it was the expression of a genuine relationship with God.

One of the most powerful aspects of Psalm 13 is the way it ends. After expressing his disappointment and anguish, David shifts his focus back to trust. In verses 5 and 6 he declares, "But I trust in your unfailing love; my heart rejoices in your salvation. I will sing the Lord's praise, for he has been good to me."

Think about the significance of that moment. David was still in the cave. His circumstances had not yet changed. Saul was still searching for him. Yet despite all of that, David chose to trust in God's faithfulness.

The cave was not where David expected to be, but it was exactly where God was preparing him for what lay ahead. The darkness of that season was shaping the future king in ways that comfort and success never could.

Many people today experience their own "cave seasons." These are periods when life feels uncertain, when prayers seem unanswered, and when the future appears unclear. It may feel as though God has gone silent or forgotten about the promises once spoken over our lives.

But silence does not mean abandonment. Often, God performs His deepest work during the quietest seasons. Just as a seed grows beneath the soil long before it breaks through the surface, spiritual growth often happens in ways we cannot immediately see.

Romans 8:24–25 reminds believers of this truth. The passage explains that hope requires patience. If we already possessed everything we hoped for, there would be no need for faith. But when we wait for what we do not yet see, we learn to trust God's timing rather than our own understanding.

The cave, therefore, is not the end of the story. It is part of the process. It is a place where God strengthens faith, deepens character, and prepares us for the responsibilities that lie ahead.

There is another remarkable detail about David's time in the Cave of Adullam. According to 1 Samuel 22, David was not alone in that place for long. Others who were distressed, discouraged, or struggling in their own lives began to gather around him. These men, many of whom were considered outcasts by society, eventually became the mighty warriors who stood beside David during his reign.

In other words, God was not only preparing David—He was also building a community through shared hardship. What began as a gathering of broken and discouraged individuals eventually became one of the most loyal and courageous groups of men in Israel's history.

This truth carries an important message for anyone walking through a difficult season. The pain we experience does not have to remain meaningless. When we allow God to work through our struggles, He can use those experiences to encourage and strengthen others who are facing similar challenges.

God has a remarkable ability to transform places of suffering into places of growth and purpose. The cave that once symbolized fear and uncertainty can eventually become the birthplace of strength, leadership, and renewed faith.

If you find yourself in a "cave season" right now—waiting, hurting, and wondering what God is doing—remember David's example. Continue to trust, even when the future is unclear. Continue to speak honestly with God about your struggles.

And just as David declared in Psalm 13, hold on to the truth that God's love remains faithful. Even in the darkest moments, He is still at work, preparing something far greater than we can see in the present.

Chapter Four Reflection – *The Battle Within*

The greatest battles many of us will ever face are not fought on a battlefield or in the middle of an emergency call. They are fought quietly within the mind and heart. For first responders, veterans, and anyone who has endured trauma, the internal struggle can sometimes feel more exhausting than the external battles we once faced.

Chapter Four reminds us that the internal fight is real. PTSD, anxiety, intrusive memories, and emotional wounds can create a constant tension between the person we once were and the person we feel we have become. The mind wants peace, yet the memories keep us alert. The heart longs for connection, yet fear or exhaustion pushes us toward isolation.

In these moments it can feel as though the battle will never end. Some may begin to question their strength or wonder why healing feels so difficult. Yet Scripture reminds us that internal conflict is not a new experience. Even great leaders of faith wrestled with discouragement, fear, and moments of despair.

The apostle Paul spoke openly about the struggle between what he wanted to do and what he sometimes found himself doing instead. The prophet Elijah once sat alone in a cave convinced that he was the only one left serving God. David cried out in frustration, asking the Lord how long his suffering would continue. These were not weak individuals; they were people who carried great responsibility and experienced deep spiritual battles.

Their stories remind us of an important truth: struggling does not mean we have failed. It simply means we are human. What matters most is not whether the battle exists, but whether we choose to continue fighting.

The fight matters because our lives matter. The effort to pursue healing matters for our families, for the people who love us, and for the purpose God has placed on our lives. Even when progress feels slow, every step forward is meaningful.

Another important truth revealed in this chapter is that isolation is one of the enemy's most effective tools. Trauma often convinces us that no one understands what we are experiencing. Yet the reality is that many others have walked similar paths. God also places people in our lives—family members, friends, counselors, mentors, and fellow believers—who are willing to walk beside us if we allow them.

Just as Elijah discovered in the cave, the feeling of being alone does not mean that we truly are. God's presence remains constant, even during the moments when we feel most abandoned. Often His voice is not heard in the chaos of life but in the quiet moments when we pause long enough to listen.

Chapter Four also reminds us that the end of one mission does not mean the end of purpose. Many first responders and veterans struggle when their season of service ends. The structure, camaraderie, and urgency that once defined daily life can disappear almost overnight. Yet God's calling on our lives is never limited to a single role or career.

Just as Elijah was given a new assignment and David was prepared for leadership during his time in the cave, our seasons of struggle can become seasons of preparation. The experiences we have endured—both the victories and the wounds—can eventually become tools that help others find hope and healing.

The cave is not the end of the story. It is often the place where God begins shaping something new. What feels like isolation may actually be preparation. What feels like silence may actually be the moment when God is doing His deepest work within us.

The battle within may be difficult, but it is not without purpose. And as long as we continue trusting God and taking one step forward at a time, the story He is writing in our lives is far from finished.

A Small Prayer

Lord,

You see the battles that take place within my heart and mind. You know the memories, fears, and struggles that I carry, even the ones I rarely speak about.

When the fight feels overwhelming, remind me that I do not face it alone. Give me the strength to keep moving forward, even on the days when progress feels small.

Help me to trust that You are still working in my life, even during the quiet seasons when I cannot clearly see what You are doing. Teach me to bring my pain, my questions, and my doubts to You honestly, just as David and Elijah did.

Surround me with people who will support me, encourage me, and walk beside me during this journey. And remind me that the purpose You placed on my life has not ended.

Use even my struggles to bring hope and healing to others. Amen.

Practical Takeaway - *Do not fight the internal battle alone.*

One of the most important steps toward healing is allowing others to walk alongside you. Isolation may feel safe, but connection often brings the support and perspective we need to move forward.

This week, consider taking one intentional step toward connection:

1. **Reach out to one trusted person.** This could be a friend, family member, fellow veteran or first responder, pastor, or counselor.

2. **Share honestly.** You do not need to tell your entire story at once. Simply begin by expressing how you have been feeling lately.

3. **Spend a few quiet moments with God each day.** Even five minutes of prayer or reflection can help calm the mind and remind you of His presence.

4. **Take the battle one step at a time.** Healing rarely happens all at once, but consistent small steps can lead to meaningful change.

Remember: continuing the fight is not a sign of weakness. It is a sign of courage. And every step forward—no matter how small—is part of the journey toward healing.

The Cost of THE CALL
Finding Healing from PTSD in Christ

This area is designated for writing notes:

IS THERE NOT A CAUSE?

"Let us not grow weary in well-doing, for in due time we will reap a harvest if we do not give up."

GALATIANS 6:9

Every great moment in life often begins with a single second of courage. It is rarely a dramatic or perfectly planned event. More often, it is a quiet decision made in the heart—one moment when a person chooses faith instead of fear, courage instead of retreat, purpose instead of despair. Those moments may seem small at the time, yet they can shape the direction of a person's life for years to come. The choices we make today inevitably influence the life we live tomorrow.

The Cost of THE CALL

Finding Healing from PTSD in Christ

Each of us, at different points in our lives, must face a defining question: will we allow our weaknesses and struggles to determine who we become, or will we trust God and rise above the storms that confront us? The answer to that question is not always easy. When someone is battling trauma, exhaustion, or discouragement, the path of surrender can appear far more attractive than the path of perseverance. Yet it is precisely in those difficult moments that character is formed and purpose is revealed.

Throughout Scripture, we see examples of individuals who reached a moment when they had to decide whether fear or faith would guide their actions. One of the most powerful examples of this can be found in the story of David and Goliath. While most people remember the dramatic image of the young shepherd defeating a towering giant with a sling and a stone, the real battle was not fought in the valley where the armies stood facing one another. The true victory had already taken place inside David's heart long before he stepped onto that battlefield.

In 1 Samuel 17, David arrives at the camp of the Israelite army. His father had sent him there with food for his brothers, who were serving in King Saul's army. When David arrived, he witnessed a scene that had become routine for the soldiers of Israel. Every day the Philistine champion, Goliath, would step forward and challenge the Israelites to send a warrior to fight him. For forty days the giant mocked the people of God and defied the armies of Israel. Each time he appeared, fear spread throughout the camp. Not a single soldier was willing to face him.

David's older brother Eliab quickly grew irritated when he saw David asking questions about the situation. He accused David of pride and questioned why he had even come to the battlefield. Eliab assumed David was simply being reckless or looking for attention. But David responded with a question that reveals the heart behind his actions. In 1 Samuel 17:29 he said, "What have I now done? Is there not a cause?"

Those five words carry profound meaning. David was not seeking recognition, and he was certainly not motivated by arrogance. What stirred his heart was something far deeper. David understood that this situation was about more than a military conflict. It was about the honor of God. The giant standing in the valley was openly defying the Lord and mocking His people, and David could not remain silent while that happened.

What made David different from everyone else present that day was not his physical strength or his military experience. In fact, compared to the seasoned soldiers around him, David appeared completely unqualified. He was young, inexperienced in warfare, and far smaller than the enemy he would eventually face. Yet David possessed something that the others had lost—faith in the power and faithfulness of God.

While the rest of Israel focused on the size of the giant, David focused on the greatness of God. Where others saw an impossible threat, David saw an opportunity for God to demonstrate His power. He refused to allow fear to dictate his response. Instead, he viewed the moment through the lens of faith.

That is why the battle had already been won before David ever picked up a stone. The victory began when he chose to believe that God was greater than the obstacle standing before him. The external confrontation in the valley was simply the visible result of an internal conviction that had already taken root in his heart.

For many veterans and first responders, life can feel like standing in that same valley. The giants we face may not carry swords or wear armor, but they can be just as intimidating. Trauma, anxiety, depression, and memories that refuse to fade can loom over us like towering enemies. They whisper lies that tell us the fight is pointless or that the battle cannot be won.

Yet the question David asked thousands of years ago still echoes today: "Is there not a cause?"

Is there not a reason to continue fighting for healing, even when the process feels slow and exhausting? Is there not a purpose in pushing forward when every part of us feels tempted to give up?

For many, the answer begins with the people we love. Our families, our spouses, our children, and our friends are deeply affected by the choices we make. Choosing to pursue healing is not only a personal decision—it is also a commitment to those who walk beside us in life.

But the cause extends even further than that. As believers, we recognize that our lives ultimately belong to God. Our struggles, our victories, and even our scars can become testimonies that point others toward Him. The battles we fight today may one day become the very stories that give someone else the courage to keep going.

David stood before Goliath because he believed there was a cause worth fighting for. He believed the honor of God and the future of his people were worth the risk.

In the same way, when we face the internal battles of life, we must remind ourselves that there is still a purpose ahead of us. Our struggles do not erase our calling. Our pain does not eliminate our value. And our past does not determine the final outcome of our story.

Sometimes all it takes is one moment of courage—one decision to trust God again, one step forward instead of backward, one prayer spoken in faith rather than silence.

Because when we begin to ask the question David asked— "Is there not a cause?"—we often rediscover the strength to keep fighting.

BACKUP

Anyone who has ever been in a dangerous situation understands the importance of backup. In a firefight or critical incident, when ammunition is running low, fatigue is setting in, and the situation seems overwhelming, the arrival of backup can change everything. The moment additional support arrives, the atmosphere shifts. What once felt hopeless suddenly becomes manageable. Strength is renewed, focus returns, and the burden that once seemed unbearable is now shared.

Backup does more than simply add numbers to a difficult situation—it restores confidence and perspective. Knowing that others have arrived to stand beside you reminds you that you are not fighting alone. In those moments, the weight of the battle becomes lighter because the responsibility is no longer resting solely on your shoulders.

The same principle applies to life. Every person, at some point, experiences fatigue. Sometimes it is physical exhaustion brought on by long hours, sleepless nights, and demanding responsibilities. Other times it is mental fatigue caused by constant stress, trauma, or the accumulation of difficult experiences over time. And perhaps the most difficult form of exhaustion is spiritual fatigue, when a person feels emotionally drained and begins to wonder if they have the strength to keep going.

Fatigue rarely arrives all at once. It builds slowly, often unnoticed at first. One difficult day becomes another, then another, until the weight of everything begins to press down on the soul. Eventually, a person may reach a point where they feel completely depleted, unsure whether they can continue moving forward.

Even some of the strongest individuals in Scripture experienced this kind of exhaustion. One powerful example can be found in the life of the prophet Elijah.

Elijah found himself running for his life. Queen Jezebel, enraged by the defeat of the prophets of Baal, threatened to kill him. Fear and exhaustion overwhelmed Elijah, and he fled into the wilderness. Eventually, he came to a place where his strength was completely gone.

The Cost of THE CALL
Finding Healing from PTSD in Christ

First Kings 19:4 describes the moment when Elijah sat down under a broom tree and poured out his despair before God. In his exhaustion he prayed, "It is enough; now, O LORD, take away my life, for I am no better than my fathers." In that moment Elijah felt defeated, isolated, and completely drained. The prophet who had just witnessed a miraculous victory now believed he had reached the end of his strength.

But God did not abandon Elijah in that moment of weakness.

Instead, God sent help.

The Bible tells us that an angel came and ministered to Elijah. The angel woke him, provided food and water, and allowed him to rest. After Elijah slept again, the angel returned a second time and encouraged him to eat once more, because the journey ahead would be too great for him to complete on his own strength.

The care God showed Elijah in that moment is deeply meaningful. Before correcting him, before redirecting him, before speaking to him about his mission, God first restored his strength. Elijah needed rest, nourishment, and encouragement before he could continue.

The Scripture tells us that after receiving this provision, Elijah traveled on the strength of that food for forty days and forty nights until he reached Mount Horeb, the same place where Moses once encountered God and received the Ten Commandments.

This story reminds us of an important truth: God understands human exhaustion. He knows that even the strongest people will eventually reach moments where they feel overwhelmed. Rather than condemning us in those moments, God often provides the support we need to continue.

Sometimes that support comes in ways we do not expect.

While we may not see angels appear as Elijah did, God often sends backup in other forms. It may be a spouse who listens when we are struggling. It may be a close friend who refuses to let us isolate ourselves. It might be a fellow veteran, a trusted counselor, or a spiritual mentor who understands the battle we are facing.

At times, backup can come through a simple conversation, a phone call at the right moment, or someone reminding us that we are not alone in our struggle.

Scripture beautifully captures this idea in Psalm 23. The psalmist writes that the Lord "makes me lie down in green pastures" and "leads me beside the still waters." These images describe rest and restoration. God does not merely push His people forward endlessly; He leads them into places where their souls can be renewed. The purpose of that rest is clear: "He restores my soul."

Restoration is not weakness. In fact, it is often the very thing that allows us to continue the journey. When we allow God to restore us—through rest, through prayer, through the support of others—we gain the strength necessary to face the next season of life.

There is also another powerful aspect to this principle. The backup we receive today may prepare us to become someone else's backup tomorrow.

Many veterans and first responders know the value of having someone who shows up when things get difficult. The encouragement we receive during our lowest moments often shapes the way we help others later in life. What God uses to restore us can eventually become a tool we use to lift someone else up.

In Ecclesiastes 4:9–10, Scripture reminds us that "two are better than one, because they have a good reward for their labor. For if they fall, one will lift up his companion. But woe to him who is alone when he falls, for he has no one to help him up."

THE LORD PROVIDES

Loneliness is a reality that many veterans and first responders know all too well. There are moments when the noise of the world fades, yet the thoughts within grow louder. Seasons of uncertainty can feel isolating, as if you are walking through a dark place with no clear direction and no one who truly understands what you are carrying. Even when surrounded by others, there can still be a deep sense of being alone in the struggle.

This feeling is not new, nor is it unique to our time. Scripture reveals that even some of God's most faithful servants experienced seasons of isolation and uncertainty. David, long before he became king, endured such a season while fleeing from King Saul. Though he had been anointed by God, his life did not immediately reflect that promise. Instead of sitting on a throne, David found himself running for his life, hiding in wilderness places, and constantly looking over his shoulder.

It would have been easy for David to believe that he had been abandoned—by people and perhaps even by God. Yet in the midst of that dark and uncertain season, God provided something that many people often overlook or even resist when they are struggling. God provided David with a friend.

Jonathan, the son of King Saul, became one of the greatest sources of support in David's life. At a time when David could trust very few people, Jonathan stood beside him with loyalty, courage, and selflessness. Their relationship was not built on convenience or circumstance, but on a deep bond that God Himself had established.

The Bible tells us that Jonathan and David formed a covenant, a commitment rooted in mutual love and respect. Jonathan, though the rightful heir to the throne as Saul's son, recognized God's calling on David's life. In a powerful act of humility and loyalty, he gave David his royal robe, armor, and weapons. This was more than a symbolic gesture—it was an acknowledgment that God's plan was greater than personal ambition.

Jonathan did not allow jealousy or fear to influence his actions. Instead, he chose faithfulness.

Even when his own father, King Saul, was consumed with jealousy and sought to kill David, Jonathan remained steadfast. He spoke on David's behalf, advocating for him and reminding Saul of David's loyalty and service. For a time, this intervention even brought a temporary peace. But Jonathan's support did not end there.

When Saul's intentions became clear once again, Jonathan warned David, helping him escape danger. He risked his own safety and position to protect his friend. Standing with David meant opposing the will of his own father, the king. Yet Jonathan chose righteousness and loyalty over comfort and security.

Their friendship stands as one of the most powerful examples of loyalty and selflessness found in Scripture. It reminds us that even in our most difficult seasons, God often works through people to provide the strength and encouragement we need.

However, there is an important truth we must recognize: while God provides support, we must be willing to receive it.

Many people, especially those who have served in high-stress environments, struggle with this. There is a tendency to rely solely on personal strength, to push through pain in silence, and to avoid opening up to others. Over time, this can lead to deeper isolation, even when help is available. Yet God never intended for us to walk through life alone.

As we have seen in earlier chapters, support can come in many forms. It may come through a fellow veteran who understands the weight of shared experiences. It may come through a spouse who stands faithfully beside us. It might be a trusted friend, a counselor, a pastor, or a mentor who listens without judgment and offers guidance when we feel lost.

The form may vary, but the source remains the same—God is the one who provides.

Even in the New Testament, we see this principle clearly demonstrated. When Jesus sent out His disciples to minister and spread the good news, He did not send them alone. In Mark 6:7, He sent them out two by two. This was not coincidence; it was intentional. Traveling in pairs provided support, accountability, and strength. It ensured that no one had to carry the burden alone.

Throughout Scripture, we see this pattern repeated. God gave Paul a Timothy—a faithful companion and spiritual son who would stand with him in ministry. He gave Elijah an Elisha—a successor and supporter who would continue the work and walk alongside him. He gave David a Jonathan—a loyal friend who strengthened him during one of the most difficult seasons of his life.

Just as God provided for them, He continues to provide for us today. The challenge, however, is not whether God will provide. The challenge is whether we will be open to receiving that provision. Support does not always look the way we expect it to, and it may require vulnerability, humility, and trust to accept it.

Allowing someone to walk alongside us in our struggles is not a sign of weakness—it is a step toward healing.

There may come a time when you find yourself at your lowest point, feeling as though you have nothing left to give. In those moments, remember that God often sends help in the form of people. Someone willing to listen, to stand with you, to remind you that you are not alone in the fight.

As you continue on your journey, you may one day find yourself in the position to be that person for someone else. The same support that helps restore you can become the very thing you offer to others.

The Lord provides—faithfully, consistently, and often in ways we do not immediately recognize. Our role is to remain open, to receive what He sends, and to keep moving forward in faith, trusting that even in our darkest moments, we are never truly alone.

Victory is not only possible—it is already being prepared, one step at a time.

KEEP GOING FOWARD

The journey of healing is not a straight path, nor is it a quick one. It is often marked by progress, setbacks, moments of clarity, and seasons of struggle. During this process, one of the most important decisions you will make is the decision not to give up prematurely. Healing requires persistence. It requires patience. And above all, it requires a willingness to keep moving forward, even when the path ahead is unclear.

Scripture offers a powerful reminder in Galatians 6:9: "Let us not grow weary in doing good, for in due season we shall reap, if we do not give up." This promise is both simple and profound. It acknowledges that weariness will come. It recognizes that doing what is right, especially in the midst of pain, is not always easy. Yet it also assures us that perseverance produces a harvest.

The principle of sowing and reaping is one that we see not only in Scripture but also in everyday life. A farmer understands that the harvest does not appear overnight. There is a season of preparation, a season of planting, a season of waiting, and finally, a season of reaping. If a farmer plants corn, he expects to harvest corn. If he plants melons, he expects melons. The harvest will always reflect the seed that was sown.

In the same way, the seeds we plant in our lives during difficult seasons will eventually produce results. The thoughts we entertain, the habits we develop, the people we surround ourselves with, and the choices we make all contribute to what we will experience later on. If we consistently sow seeds of negativity, isolation, and hopelessness, those are the fruits we will eventually see. But if we sow seeds of faith, truth, discipline, and hope, we begin to cultivate a life that leads toward healing and restoration.

It is important to be honest about the reality of this journey. There will be days when everything feels dark and overwhelming. There will be moments when it seems as though nothing is changing, when progress feels slow, and when discouragement begins to creep in. There may even be times when it feels like everything—and everyone—is working against you. Those are the moments that matter most.

It is in those moments that you must choose to dig deep. Not by relying solely on your own strength, but by placing your trust in God and in His Word. Feelings can be powerful, but they are not always reliable. Circumstances can appear overwhelming, but they do not define the final outcome. Faith calls us to look beyond what we see and to trust in what God has promised.

Hebrews 10:39 reminds us of this truth: "But we are not of those who shrink back and are destroyed, but of those who believe and are saved." This verse draws a clear line between retreat and perseverance. To shrink back is to allow fear, doubt, or exhaustion to dictate our decisions. To persevere is to continue moving forward, even when the journey is difficult.

Healing requires intentionality. It requires that we actively sow into our lives things that will bring growth rather than harm. This may include spending time in prayer, meditating on Scripture, seeking wise counsel, engaging in healthy relationships, and making choices that support both mental and spiritual well-being.

What we allow into our minds matters. The words we listen to, the thoughts we dwell on, and the beliefs we hold will shape our perspective and influence our actions. When we meditate on the Word of God, we are not simply reading words on a page—we are engaging with truth that has the power to transform us from the inside out. Scripture brings life, clarity, and direction, especially in times when confusion and doubt try to take hold.

The early disciples understood what it meant to persevere in the face of opposition. They faced persecution, rejection, and hardship, yet they continued to move forward with boldness and faith. What gave them that strength was not their own ability, but the presence of Christ within them. Through the Holy Spirit, they were empowered to endure, to continue, and to fulfill the calling placed on their lives.

The same power that sustained them is available to us today. Jesus Himself made this clear in Matthew 19:26 when He said, "With man this is impossible, but with God all things are possible." On our own, the journey may feel overwhelming. The weight of trauma, the difficulty of healing, and the challenges of daily life can seem too much to carry. But with God, what appears impossible becomes possible.

Progress may not always be visible, but that does not mean it is not happening. Growth often takes place beneath the surface, much like a seed planted in the ground. For a time, nothing seems to change. Yet beneath the soil, roots are forming, strength is developing, and life is preparing to emerge.

In the same way, God is at work even when we cannot see it. So keep going forward. Keep choosing faith over fear. Keep planting seeds that will lead to life. Keep trusting that the work God has started in you is not finished. Every step forward, no matter how small, is a step in the right direction.

You may not feel strong every day, but strength is not always about how you feel—it is about the decision to keep moving forward despite those feelings. And as long as you continue to take those steps, trusting God along the way, you are already closer to the healing and restoration that awaits you.

YOU GOT THIS!

God is not finished with you yet. No matter how long the road has been or how heavy the burden has felt, your story is still being written. Scripture reminds us that God is both the Author and the Finisher of our faith, and the work He has begun in your life, He is faithful to complete. What may feel unfinished, broken, or delayed is still under His authority and care.

There is a powerful truth found throughout Scripture: what was meant for harm, God can turn for good. This does not mean that the pain was necessary or that the trauma was insignificant. It means that God, in His sovereignty, is able to take even the darkest moments of our lives and use them to produce something meaningful, something redemptive, and something that can ultimately bring healing—not only to us, but to others as well.

Consider everything you have already endured. The long hours of training, the discipline required to prepare for the unknown, the sleepless nights, and the physical and emotional demands of service. The double shifts, the deployments, the moments spent in dangerous environments where uncertainty was the only constant. The calls that stayed with you long after they ended. The faces you cannot forget. The partners, friends, and colleagues lost along the way. Each of these experiences leaves an imprint, shaping not only your memory but your entire being.

Add to that the weight of trauma—physical, emotional, and mental—that often goes unseen by others. These are burdens that many carry silently, unsure of how to express what they have experienced or how to process what they have seen. It is a weight that cannot always be explained, only felt. And yet, none of it is without purpose.

While it may not always be clear in the moment, God does not waste pain. Every experience, every hardship, and every battle can be used as part of a greater work that He is doing in and through your life.

At the same time, it is important to recognize that there is also a real spiritual battle taking place. Scripture teaches that there is an enemy who seeks to destroy, discourage, and devour. First Peter 5:8 warns us to be alert and sober-minded because our adversary, the devil, prowls around like a roaring lion, looking for someone to devour.

This enemy does not operate randomly. His strategies are intentional. His goal is not only to create chaos in our lives but to weaken our identity, distort our thinking, and separate us from the truth of who we are in Christ. John 10:10 makes this clear: the enemy comes to steal, kill, and destroy. His aim is destruction—emotionally, mentally, spiritually, and ultimately eternally.

One of the ways this battle plays out is in the mind. Thoughts can become strongholds if left unchecked. Fear, guilt, shame, anger, and hopelessness can begin to take root and shape the way we see ourselves and the world around us. Over time, these thoughts can influence our decisions and behaviors, creating patterns that are difficult to break.

Ephesians 4:27 instructs us not to give the enemy a foothold. In other words, we are not to allow space in our lives for destructive patterns, thoughts, or behaviors to take control. The enemy often works through our weaknesses and our fallen nature, exploiting areas where we are already vulnerable.

There is a parallel here that is important to recognize. Just as negative patterns can gain strength when they are fed, healing and restoration grow stronger when we actively pursue what is good, true, and life-giving. The more we resist destructive thoughts and replace them with truth, the more we weaken their hold over us. This is why the battle in the mind is so significant.

Just as David defeated Goliath internally before he ever stepped onto the battlefield, we too can experience victory in our daily lives by aligning our thoughts with God's truth. Victory begins with surrender—not surrender to defeat, but surrender to God.

James 4:7 provides a clear strategy: "Submit yourselves, then, to God. Resist the devil, and he will flee from you." Notice the order. First comes submission to God—aligning our hearts, minds, and lives with Him. Then comes resistance. When we stand firm in that position, the enemy loses ground.

It is important to understand that this is not merely a physical or emotional battle. It is also spiritual. Second Corinthians 10:4 reminds us that the weapons we fight with are not of this world. They are not based on human strength or ability. Instead, they have divine power to demolish strongholds—those deeply rooted patterns of thinking and belief that keep us stuck.

God has not left us unprotected in this battle. In Ephesians 6:10–18, we are given a picture of the armor of God—a complete set of spiritual protection designed to help us stand firm. Truth, righteousness, peace, faith, salvation, and the Word of God are not abstract ideas; they are essential tools for daily living.

The belt of truth holds everything together, reminding us of what is real and unchanging. The breastplate of righteousness protects our identity in Christ. The gospel of peace steadies our steps. The shield of faith guards us against the attacks that come our way. The helmet of salvation protects our minds, and the sword of the Spirit—the Word of God—equips us to respond with truth. And over all of this, we are called to pray—continually, honestly, and faithfully. This is how we stand.

There will still be difficult days. There will still be moments when the battle feels intense. But you are not fighting alone, and you are not fighting without purpose.

Everything you have endured, everything you have overcome, and everything you are still working through is part of a larger story that God is unfolding.

So keep going.

Keep standing.

Keep trusting.

Because no matter how hard the battle may feel right now, one truth remains:

You've got this—not because of your own strength alone, but because God is with you, working in you, and fighting for you every step of the way.

Chapter 5 Reflection - *Is There Not a Cause?*

There comes a moment in every life when we are faced with a defining question: *Why does this matter?* In the midst of pain, fatigue, and ongoing battles—whether internal or external—it can be easy to lose sight of purpose. Like David standing before Goliath, we may find ourselves surrounded by voices of doubt, fear, and even criticism. Yet David saw something others did not. He saw a cause worth standing for.

This chapter challenges us to shift our perspective. Instead of focusing solely on the size of the "giants" we face—trauma, fear, PTSD, loss—we are invited to focus on the purpose behind the fight. There is a reason to keep going. There is a reason to stand. There is a reason to believe that your life still holds meaning beyond the pain.

"Is there not a cause?" is more than a question—it is a call to action. It is a reminder that your life has value, that your story matters, and that your perseverance can impact others in ways you may never fully see. Your fight is not just for survival—it is for restoration, for your family, for those watching your journey, and ultimately for God's glory.

Even when you feel overlooked, misunderstood, or weary, there is still a cause. The question is not whether the cause exists—the question is whether we will rise up and answer it.

Prayer

Heavenly Father,

Thank You for reminding me that my life has purpose, even in the midst of struggle. When I feel overwhelmed, tired, or discouraged, help me to see beyond my circumstances and recognize the greater cause You have placed before me.

Give me the courage to stand firm, just as David did, even when others doubt me or when fear tries to take hold of my heart. Strengthen my faith so that I do not focus on the size of the battle, but on the greatness of who You are.

Lord, help me to trust that nothing I have gone through is wasted. Use my life, my story, and even my pain to bring glory to You and to help others who may be struggling.

Remind me daily that there is a cause worth fighting for.

In Jesus' name, Amen.

Practical Takeaway

Ask yourself one simple but powerful question each day: ***"What is my cause today?"***

Your cause does not always have to be something big or dramatic. Some days, your cause may simply be getting out of bed, choosing hope over despair, or reaching out to someone you trust. Other days, it may be encouraging a fellow veteran, being present for your family, or continuing your healing journey when it feels difficult.

Write it down. Be intentional. When you feel overwhelmed, come back to that purpose and let it ground you.

Also, identify one "giant" you are currently facing and reframe it. Instead of asking, *"Why is this happening to me?"* ask, *"What is God trying to do through this?"*

Finally, surround yourself with reminders of your purpose—Scripture, supportive people, and daily habits that reinforce truth. Purpose fuels perseverance. When you know your "why," you are far more likely to keep going, no matter how difficult the battle becomes.

Because there *is* a cause—and your life is part of it.

THE ANSWER

"I am the way and the truth and the life. No one comes to the Father except through me."

JOHN 14:6

God never intended for us to navigate life on our own. From the very beginning, His design was for relationship, guidance, and dependence on Him. In a world filled with uncertainty, pain, and confusion, He has not left us without direction. Instead, He has given us a roadmap—not only for how to live, but for how to heal, endure, and ultimately find eternal hope. That roadmap is His Word.

Scripture describes the Word of God as "a lamp unto my feet and a light unto my path" (Psalm 119:105). This imagery is both practical and profound. A lamp does not illuminate the entire journey at once; it provides just enough light for the next step. In the same way, God often guides us one step at a time. For those walking through the darkness of trauma, anxiety, or PTSD, this truth is essential. Healing is not always immediate or linear, but God's Word provides steady guidance, illuminating each step forward even when the full path is not yet visible.

One of the greatest sources of comfort found in Scripture is the assurance that God fully sees and understands us. Psalm 139:1–4 reveals a deeply personal truth: God knows us intimately. He knows our thoughts before we speak them, our actions before we take them, and our struggles before we can even articulate them. For those carrying invisible wounds— memories, triggers, emotional pain—this truth is powerful. You are not overlooked. You are not misunderstood. You are fully known by God.

This awareness is not distant or impersonal. It is rooted in His presence. God is not observing from afar; He is actively involved in our lives. He walks with us through every valley, every moment of fear, and every season of uncertainty. For individuals dealing with the lingering effects of trauma, this means that even in the most isolating moments, you are not alone. His presence is constant, even when it is not always felt.

What makes this truth even more powerful is that God does not merely understand us from a position of authority—He understands us through experience. Through Jesus Christ, God stepped into human existence. He became fully human and willingly entered into suffering.

Hebrews 2:17–18 reminds us that Jesus was made like us in every way so that He could become a merciful and faithful High Priest. Because He Himself suffered and was tempted, He is able to help those who are suffering and being tempted. This is not theoretical empathy—it is lived experience.

Hebrews 4:15 reinforces this truth: we do not have a High Priest who is unable to empathize with our weaknesses, but One who has been tempted in every way, just as we are—yet without sin. Jesus understands exhaustion. He understands grief. He understands betrayal, abandonment, rejection, and physical suffering.

He knows what it feels like to be misunderstood by those closest to Him. He knows what it is like to face overwhelming anguish, as seen in the Garden of Gethsemane. He knows what it is like to endure physical pain, humiliation, and injustice.

Because of this, when we bring our pain to Him, we are not speaking to someone who is distant or disconnected—we are speaking to someone who truly understands.

For those struggling with PTSD, this truth carries deep significance. Trauma often brings feelings of isolation, as if no one else could possibly understand what you have experienced. But Christ does. He meets you in that place—not with judgment, but with compassion, mercy, and grace.

The Apostle Paul offers another perspective that is essential to understanding healing through Christ. In Romans 5:3–5, he writes that we can rejoice in our sufferings—not because suffering itself is good, but because of what God produces through it. Suffering develops perseverance; perseverance builds character; and character strengthens hope.

This does not minimize the reality of pain. Rather, it reframes it. Pain is no longer meaningless—it becomes part of a process through which God refines, strengthens, and transforms us. For those on the path of healing, this means that even the hardest days are not wasted. God is working, even when the progress feels slow or invisible.

Healing from trauma often involves rebuilding—rebuilding trust, identity, and a sense of safety. In Christ, this rebuilding is anchored in truth. Your identity is not defined by what happened to you, but by who God says you are. You are not your trauma. You are not your past. You are a new creation in Him, being restored day by day.

When we align ourselves with God's will, we begin to see our lives through a different lens. Our suffering is no longer in vain. It becomes part of a greater purpose—one that can bring healing not only to ourselves, but also to others who are walking a similar path.

There may be moments when it feels like God is distant, when prayers seem unanswered, or when the weight of your struggle feels too heavy to carry. But God's promises remain true regardless of how we feel in the moment. He has said that He will never leave us nor forsake us (Hebrews 13:5). He invites us to draw near to Him with the assurance that He will draw near to us (James 4:8).

This is the answer—not a quick fix, not an easy path, but a relationship with a faithful God who walks with us through every step of the healing journey.

He sees you.

He understands you.

And He is not finished with you yet.

ANSWERING THE CALL

There is a condition that runs far deeper than any physical or psychological wound we may carry. While trauma, stress, and emotional pain are real and significant, Scripture reveals that the root issue of humanity is spiritual in nature. The Bible calls this condition sin. From the moment of the fall in the Garden of Eden, when Adam and Eve chose disobedience, humanity's relationship with God was fractured. As a result, every person born into this world inherits a fallen nature. Psalm 51:5 expresses this truth clearly—that we are born into sin, shaped by a condition that separates us from a holy and perfect God.

This separation is not merely theological; it is deeply personal. It affects how we think, how we live, how we relate to others, and how we understand ourselves. It contributes to the brokenness we experience in the world and within our own hearts. While trauma and PTSD may shape our experiences and responses, sin affects the core of who we are. Left unaddressed, it creates a barrier between us and the very source of true healing and restoration—God Himself. Yet this is precisely why Jesus came.

Jesus Christ entered into our broken world with a clear mission: to restore what had been lost. Through His life, death, and resurrection, He made a way for that broken relationship between humanity and God to be healed. The cross was not only an act of sacrifice—it was an act of reconciliation. Because of what Jesus accomplished, we are no longer separated from God. We are invited into a restored relationship with Him.

It is important to understand that while physical and emotional healing are vital, they are not the ultimate solution. The deeper need is spiritual transformation. The problem is not only what has happened to us—it is the condition of the human heart. This is why God, through the prophet Ezekiel, promised something radical: "I will remove from you your heart of stone and give you a heart of flesh" (Ezekiel 36:26). This is not surface-level change. This is complete renewal from the inside out.

God's desire is not simply to improve our lives, but to transform them. He wants to restore us spiritually, to give us new life, new desires, and a new direction. This transformation is essential in the journey of healing from trauma. While therapy, support systems, and practical steps are important, true and lasting healing begins with a renewed heart—one that is aligned with God.

Isaiah 53:5 declares, "By His stripes we are healed." This healing is comprehensive. It speaks not only to physical healing, but to spiritual and emotional restoration as well. Jesus bore our sins, our brokenness, and our suffering so that we could be made whole. Through Him, healing is not just possible—it is promised to those who come to Him in faith.

The pathway to this transformation is clearly illustrated in the Gospel of John. In chapter 3, a Pharisee named Nicodemus comes to Jesus at night, seeking understanding. He recognizes that Jesus is from God, yet he does not fully grasp the nature of the kingdom Jesus is speaking about. Jesus responds with a statement that cuts to the core of the human condition: "Unless one is born again, he cannot see the kingdom of God."

This concept of being "born again" speaks to a spiritual rebirth. It is not about external behavior or religious performance. It is about an internal transformation brought about by the Holy Spirit. Because of our fallen nature, we cannot fully understand or follow God on our own. We need new life—a new heart, a new spirit, and a renewed mind.

This is where the Holy Spirit comes in. When we invite God into our lives, the Holy Spirit begins to dwell within us, guiding us, strengthening us, and transforming us from the inside out. In John 14, Jesus promises that God will make His home with those who love Him. This means that we are never alone in our healing journey. God is not just with us—He is within us.

It is crucial to understand that this is not about religion, tradition, or denomination. It is about relationship. Many have tried to find peace through external means—through success, distraction, or even religious activity—but true peace is only found in a genuine relationship with God through Jesus Christ.

For those struggling with PTSD and the weight of past experiences, this invitation is especially significant. You may have tried different avenues to find relief—some helpful, others not—but there remains a deeper call. God is inviting you into something greater than temporary relief. He is inviting you into transformation.

Answering this call requires surrender. It means bringing your pain, your past, your questions, and your struggles before God and allowing Him to begin a new work in you. It does not mean that everything will change overnight, but it does mean that you will no longer walk the path alone.

As you surrender your pain to Him, something remarkable begins to happen. God does not simply remove the pain—He redeems it. He begins to use your experiences, even the most difficult ones, as a means to bring healing to others. Your story becomes a testimony. Your struggle becomes a source of strength for someone else.

This is the beauty of God's work: He takes what was broken and creates something meaningful and purposeful.

The invitation is clear, and the moment is now. Scripture reminds us that "today is the day of salvation" (2 Corinthians 6:2). Hebrews warns us not to harden our hearts when we hear

His voice, as was done in the wilderness. There is urgency in this call—not out of fear, but out of opportunity.

God is calling you—not to religion, but to relationship. Not to perfection, but to transformation. Not to carry your burdens alone, but to lay them down and receive new life.

The question is not whether the call is being made.

The question is: will you answer it?

A NEW MISSION

I still remember when the call to ministry first became real in my life. In many ways, it felt similar to the calling I had experienced at a young age to serve in law enforcement. That desire—to serve, to protect, to make a difference—had always been strong within me. Yet this new calling was different. It carried a deeper weight, one that went beyond physical service and into the spiritual lives of others.

If you had asked me as a child whether I would one day become a pastor or minister, I would have laughed without hesitation. Not out of disrespect for the role, but because it seemed completely incompatible with who I was at the time. I was extremely shy. I avoided speaking whenever possible. The idea of standing before others, sharing openly and leading spiritually, felt far beyond my capabilities.

But God does not call us based on our comfort zones—He calls us according to His purpose.

When that calling came, I was still in the process of healing. I was still carrying the weight of trauma. I was still navigating the realities of PTSD, and in many ways, that journey continues even today. Healing, I have come to understand, is not always about the complete absence of struggle, but about transformation in the midst of it.

The difference now is not that every challenge has disappeared, but that my foundation has changed. There is now an assurance within me—a peace that truly surpasses understanding. It is not dependent on circumstances, emotions, or external stability. It is rooted in my relationship with God.

Scripture describes this process in 2 Corinthians 3:18, reminding us that we are being transformed "from glory to glory." This means that our growth is ongoing. Day by day, step by step, God is shaping us into the image of Christ. For those healing from trauma, this truth is incredibly important. Progress may feel slow, and setbacks may occur, but God is still working. Transformation is taking place, even when it is not immediately visible.

In the midst of that transformation, God gave me a new mission.

That mission was not separate from my pain—it was born out of it.

God began to place a burden on my heart to help others who were walking a similar path. Those struggling with trauma, those feeling lost after service, those searching for meaning beyond the uniform. The assignment was simple, yet powerful: share your story, point people to hope, and remind them that God is the answer we have all been searching for.

This is often how God works. He does not waste our experiences. Instead, He redeems them. The very areas where we have been wounded often become the places from which we can minister most effectively. What once felt like a weakness becomes a source of connection, understanding, and impact.

It is important to recognize that while our missions may differ, the message remains the same. Not everyone is called to stand behind a pulpit or write a book, but every believer is called to reflect Christ in their own sphere of influence. For some, that mission is lived out in the workplace. For others, it is within the home, the community, or among fellow veterans and first responders.

During my time in law enforcement, God allowed me to serve not only through my official duties but also through opportunities to support others in areas of resilience and mental well-being. He opened doors for conversations, for encouragement, and for moments where faith and service intersected in meaningful ways.

When I retired, I believed that chapter had come to an end. I thought that my season of active service—at least in that capacity—was over. Like many who step away from the uniform, I wrestled with questions about purpose and direction. I wondered what was next. What I did not realize was that God was not finished.

In ways I could not have predicted, He began to open new doors. He placed a desire in my heart to write, to share, and to reach others beyond the immediate circles I had once served. Through writing, I found a new avenue to minister—one that allowed me to speak into the lives of people I may never meet in person, yet who are walking similar journeys.

More recently, He has expanded that mission even further, calling me into areas such as radio ministry. Each step has been unexpected, yet clearly directed. Each opportunity has reinforced a simple truth: God's plans are often greater than anything we could imagine for ourselves.

For those navigating the effects of PTSD, this carries a powerful message of hope. Your life is not over. Your purpose has not ended. Even if one chapter has closed, God is able to begin another—one that brings healing not only to you, but also to others through you.

A new mission does not mean the absence of struggle. It means finding purpose within it. It means allowing God to take what you have experienced and use it as a tool for restoration, connection, and impact.

You may not yet see what that mission looks like in your own life. It may feel uncertain or even impossible. But when you surrender your life fully to God, you open the door for Him to work in ways you never expected.

He will guide you. He will equip you. And He will use you. Your mission may look different than mine, but it is no less significant.

In the process of fulfilling it, you may find that God is not only using you to help others—but that He is continuing to heal you along the way.

DESPITE THE PAIN

Suffering from PTSD is not a disqualification from being used by God. On the contrary, it can become one of the very avenues through which He works most powerfully. What often feels like a limitation in our lives can, in God's hands, become a bridge to reach others who are walking through similar struggles. Pain, when surrendered to Him, is never wasted.

The Cost of THE CALL
Finding Healing from PTSD in Christ

For many veterans and first responders, PTSD carries a heavy cost. It affects not only the individual but also their relationships, careers, and overall quality of life. Moments that should be filled with joy—family gatherings, celebrations, simple daily interactions—are often overshadowed by intrusive thoughts, anxiety, and emotional exhaustion. Opportunities for growth, both personally and professionally, may be missed due to the unpredictability of symptoms and the weight of internal battles.

This has been my experience as well. There have been countless times when I missed important family events, stepped away from opportunities, or withdrew from situations because of overwhelming thoughts and feelings I could not easily control. The constant alertness, the anticipation of the unknown, and the sudden triggers that bring everything rushing back can be exhausting. These moments can create a sense of frustration, guilt, and even isolation.

In those struggles, I have often found myself relating to the words of the Apostle Paul in Romans 7:24: "What a wretched man I am! Who will rescue me from this body of death?" Paul describes an internal conflict—a battle between what he desires to do and what he finds himself doing instead. For those dealing with PTSD, this resonates deeply. There is often a gap between who we want to be and how we find ourselves responding in difficult moments. But Paul does not end there. He points to the answer: Jesus Christ.

Christ has become my strength in those moments of weakness. There are times when intrusive thoughts attempt to take hold, when anxiety begins to rise, or when past experiences resurface without warning. Yet, over time, something has changed. Those thoughts no longer go unchallenged. They are met with truth.

The more time I have spent in God's Word, the more I have noticed a shift. The intrusive thoughts may still come, but they do not carry the same weight or authority. Instead, Scripture begins to rise up within me, redirecting my focus and grounding me in truth. This is not an overnight transformation, but a process—one that requires consistency, intentionality, and trust.

There is a renewing that takes place when we consistently engage with God's Word. Romans 12:2 speaks of the renewing of the mind, a process that is essential for anyone seeking healing from trauma. Our minds, shaped by past experiences, often default to patterns of fear, anxiety, or negativity. But through God's truth, those patterns can begin to change.

I have also experienced that when I submit to God—when I choose to trust Him despite how I feel—He meets me in that place. There are moments when a peace comes over me that I cannot fully explain. It is not dependent on my circumstances, nor does it mean that everything around me has suddenly changed. Rather, it is an inner calm that steadies me, allowing me to move forward and do what He has called me to do.

In those moments of obedience, something remarkable happens. What once felt like a barrier becomes an opportunity. Others are encouraged. Lives are touched. And I am reminded that God is working not only through me, but also within me.

Jesus speaks of this kind of peace in John 14:27: "Peace I leave with you; my peace I give you. I do not give to you as the world gives." The peace that the world offers is often temporary and dependent on external conditions—comfort, control, or the absence of conflict. But the peace that Christ gives is different. It is deeper. It remains even in the presence of fear, uncertainty, and pain.

For those living with PTSD, this distinction is critical. Circumstances may not always be within our control. Triggers may still exist. Difficult days may still come. But the peace of Christ is not limited by those realities. It is available in the midst of them.

Over time, as you continue to walk with Christ, this peace becomes more evident. It does not mean that the struggle disappears, but it does mean that the struggle no longer defines you. You begin to respond differently. You begin to see differently. You begin to live with a greater sense of stability and hope. And through that peace, you become a vessel for others.

There is something powerful about a person who continues to move forward despite pain. It speaks louder than words. It demonstrates resilience, faith, and authenticity. When others see that you are still standing, still trusting, and still moving forward, it gives them hope that they can do the same.

Your story, your struggles, and your perseverance become part of a greater testimony—one that God can use to reach those who may feel alone or without hope. So do not believe the lie that your pain disqualifies you.

It does not.

God can and will use you—right where you are, even in the midst of your healing journey. And as you continue to walk with Him, you will discover that it is possible to live with purpose, to serve others, and to experience His peace—

even despite the pain.

UNWAVERING SUPPORT

The New Testament uses the Greek word *agape* to describe a love that is selfless, sacrificial, and unconditional. This is the very love that God has for humanity—a love that does not waver based on circumstances, performance, or emotions. It is a steadfast, enduring love that remains present even in the most difficult seasons. This same kind of love becomes essential when supporting first responders and veterans who are struggling with PTSD.

Support is not merely helpful in the healing process—it is vital. While much of the focus is often placed on the individual experiencing trauma, it is important to recognize that healing is rarely accomplished in isolation. God designed us for relationship, for community, and for mutual support. For those who have carried the weight of the uniform, the presence of understanding, patient, and committed family members and friends can make a profound difference in their journey toward healing.

However, supporting someone with PTSD comes with a learning curve. It requires intentionality, humility, and a willingness to grow. The symptoms of trauma—such as hypervigilance, emotional withdrawal, irritability, anxiety, and avoidance—can often be misunderstood. Without proper awareness, these behaviors may be interpreted as disinterest, anger, or detachment, when in reality they are often protective responses shaped by past experiences.

At the heart of true support lies an unwavering commitment to understanding. It means choosing to remain present even when things are difficult, confusing, or emotionally taxing. It means recognizing that healing takes time and that progress is not always linear. When this kind of support is absent, it is easy for walls to form—walls of misunderstanding, frustration, and emotional distance. These barriers can create further isolation for both the individual struggling with PTSD and those trying to support them.

Yet when support is rooted in compassion, patience, and resilience, those walls can begin to break down. Over time, trust can be rebuilt, communication can improve, and relationships can grow stronger. What once felt like separation can become a source of unity and mutual strength.

For believers, this support must ultimately be grounded in God. Ecclesiastes 4:12 reminds us that "a cord of three strands is not quickly broken." When God is at the center of a relationship, there is a strength that goes beyond human effort alone. Prayer, studying God's Word together, and seeking His guidance create a spiritual foundation that sustains both individuals through the challenges of healing.

From both a spiritual and practical perspective, there are key principles that can strengthen this support system:

Communication is foundational. Healthy support begins with open and honest communication. This includes not only expressing thoughts and feelings, but also practicing active listening. At times, communication may feel one-sided, especially when the individual struggling with PTSD finds it difficult to articulate what they are experiencing. In those moments, patience and presence speak volumes. Creating a safe space where there is no judgment fosters trust and encourages openness over time.

Pursue informed understanding. PTSD is a complex condition that affects both the brain and the body. Research shows that trauma can impact the nervous system, leading to heightened states of alertness, difficulty regulating emotions, and challenges with memory and concentration. Understanding these responses as physiological and psychological—not personal failures—can shift the way support is offered. Education empowers families and friends to respond with empathy rather than frustration.

Practice balanced self-care. Supporting someone through trauma can be emotionally demanding. It is essential for caregivers, spouses, and loved ones to also care for their own mental, emotional, and spiritual health. This is not selfish—it is necessary. When you are healthy, you are better equipped to provide consistent and meaningful support. Burnout helps no one; strength is sustained through balance.

Encourage professional support. While spiritual guidance and relational support are crucial, professional care is also an important part of the healing process. Evidence-based treatments such as cognitive behavioral therapy (CBT), trauma-focused therapy, and peer support programs have been shown to be highly effective for individuals with PTSD. Encouraging a loved one to seek help should be done with gentleness and respect, never force or pressure. Professional help is not a sign of weakness—it is a step toward healing.

Build resilience through hope and community. There is great strength found in shared experiences. Connecting with other veterans, first responders, and families who have walked similar paths can provide encouragement and perspective. Many have faced the depths of trauma and have found ways to rebuild their lives. Their stories serve as reminders that healing is possible and that no one has to walk this journey alone.

It is also important to recognize that healing often occurs in layers. There may be progress in one area while another area still needs attention. There may be good days and difficult days. Through it all, unwavering support remains a constant anchor.

God's *agape* love serves as the ultimate example. It is patient, enduring, and faithful. When we reflect that love in our relationships, we create an environment where healing can take place—not perfectly, but authentically.

There is strength in unity. When individuals come together with a shared commitment to growth, understanding, and faith, something powerful begins to form. What was once fragile becomes resilient. What was once broken begins to mend.

Together, through love, faith, and intentional support, a path is created—one that leads toward healing, restoration, and a deeper, more enduring connection.

Chapter 6 Reflection - *The Answer*

Chapter 6 brings us to the most important truth in this entire journey: healing is not found in a method alone, but in a Person. For so long, many of us search for answers in different places—career, distractions, relationships, even isolation—hoping something will quiet the storm within. Yet the deeper need of the human heart is not simply relief, but restoration. That restoration is found in a relationship with God through Jesus Christ.

This chapter reminds us that God sees us fully, understands us completely, and meets us exactly where we are. He is not distant from our pain. Through Christ, He experienced suffering, rejection, betrayal, and anguish. This means that when we bring our struggles—our trauma, our anxiety, our questions—we are not bringing them to someone who is unaware, but to someone who truly understands.

The call to be "born again" is not about religion or performance; it is about transformation. It is about receiving a new heart, a renewed mind, and a restored relationship with God. This is where true healing begins. While PTSD may affect the mind and body, God works at the deepest level—the soul—bringing peace, purpose, and identity.

We also see that healing is not the end of the story—purpose is. God gives us a new mission. He takes what we have been through and uses it to reach others. The pain does not disqualify us; it becomes part of our testimony. Even "despite the pain," God can work through us, bringing hope to those who are still in the struggle.

Finally, this chapter reminds us that we are not meant to walk this journey alone. God provides support—through His presence, through His Word, and through others. Healing is strengthened in community, in relationships rooted in love, patience, and understanding.

The answer is clear: God has not abandoned you. He is calling you—into relationship, into healing, and into purpose.

Prayer

Heavenly Father,

Thank You for being the answer I have been searching for. Thank You for seeing me, understanding me, and loving me even in my brokenness.

Lord, I surrender my life to You—my past, my pain, my

struggles, and my fears. I ask that You would renew my heart and my mind. Help me to trust You in the process of healing, even when it feels slow or difficult.

Jesus, thank You for understanding my pain and for walking with me through it. Fill me with Your peace—the kind that surpasses all understanding. Strengthen me when I feel weak, and remind me that I am never alone.

Show me the purpose You have for my life. Use my story to help others, and give me the courage to step into the mission You have prepared for me.

Surround me with the right people who will support me, encourage me, and walk alongside me in this journey.

I trust You, Lord.

In Jesus' name, Amen.

Practical Takeaway

Take one intentional step toward God and one step toward support this week.

First, focus on your relationship with God:

- Set aside 10–15 minutes daily to read Scripture (start with the Gospel of John or Psalms).
- Be honest in prayer—talk to God about your struggles, not just what you think you "should" say.
- Write down one truth from God's Word each day and

reflect on it.

Second, take a step toward healing through support:

- Reach out to someone you trust—a friend, fellow veteran, pastor, or counselor.

- If you are not currently receiving professional help, consider exploring it. Healing often requires both spiritual and practical support.

- Share a small part of your story with someone safe. You do not have to carry it alone.

Finally, begin to ask yourself: **"How can God use my story to help someone else?"** You do not need to have everything figured out. You do not need to be fully healed to begin. Just be willing. Because healing starts with surrender—and purpose begins when you say yes to the call.

chapter seven

STORIES OF REDEMPTION

"They have conquered him by the blood of the Lamb and by the word of their testimony. And they did not love their lives so as to shy away from death."

REVELATION 12:11

Every battle leaves a mark. Some marks are visible—scars on the body that tell stories of sacrifice and survival. Others are invisible, carried quietly in the mind and the heart. For many veterans and first responders, the deepest wounds are the ones no one else can see.

Throughout this book we have explored the call to serve, the cost of that calling, and the internal battles that often follow. We have talked about trauma, isolation, faith, and the long journey toward healing. Yet no explanation or teaching can ever replace the power of a personal story. Testimonies matter because they remind us that we are not alone.

Behind every uniform is a human being. Behind every badge, every helmet, every rifle, and every radio is a person who has seen things most people will never see. Many have walked through moments of chaos, loss, and tragedy that permanently change the way they view the world.

Some of those moments leave behind invisible wounds— memories that replay in the quiet hours, emotions that feel difficult to explain, and questions that seem to have no easy answers. Yet even in the darkest places, God is still at work.

The testimonies in this chapter are not stories of perfect people who never struggled. They are stories of real men and women who have faced trauma, battled despair, wrestled with faith, and searched for meaning after the uniform came off.

Some of them encountered Christ in the middle of their darkest moments. Others found Him slowly, through a process of questioning, prayer, and unexpected encounters with grace.

What they all share is the realization that their pain did not have to define their future.

Jesus once said in John 8:36, "If the Son sets you free, you will be free indeed." Freedom does not mean the past disappears or that the scars vanish overnight. Rather, it means that the past no longer has the final authority over our lives.

These testimonies are living examples of that truth. They show us that healing is possible. They remind us that faith can survive even the deepest trauma. And perhaps most importantly, they reveal that God often meets people in the very places where they believed they were completely alone.

If you are reading this chapter while carrying your own unseen battles, my prayer is that these stories will encourage you. Somewhere within these testimonies you may recognize a piece of your own journey. And if you do, remember this: the same God who met these men and women in their struggles is ready to meet you in yours.

INTRODUCTION TO TESTIMONY ONE

Every journey begins somewhere. Before the uniform, before the deployments, before the late-night calls and critical incidents, there was a life being formed—dreams, family, hopes, and plans for the future. The following testimony begins with those early years and traces the path that eventually led through service, struggle, and ultimately toward faith in Christ. It is a reminder that God's story in our lives often begins long before we realize it.

Testimony one

I grew up in El Paso, Texas, in the Ysleta area. From the

outside, it may have looked like a normal upbringing, but responsibility came early for me. By the time I was five years old, I was already working in the family landscaping business. At ten, I was responsible for buying my own school supplies—clothes, paper, the basics most kids don't think twice about. That responsibility shaped me, but so did the dynamics inside my home.

My mother was a blessing. She was always present—at school events, football games, and anything that involved her kids. My father, on the other hand, was mostly present at work and often absent everywhere else. Alcohol had a strong hold on him. He tended to invest more time in my cousins, who didn't have a father, than in us. As a young man, I didn't fully understand it, but it left a mark.

We had a Catholic background, but faith was more tradition than relationship. Church was something we attended on key dates—Ash Wednesday, Easter, Christmas, and funerals. God was there, but distant.

From a young age, I knew I wanted more. I had two clear goals: to become a United States Marine and to serve in law enforcement. At seventeen, I enlisted in the Marine Corps—not just out of patriotism, but as a way to escape the environment I grew up in. I wanted to break the cycle. I wanted to become the opposite of what I had seen in my father. I wanted to serve.

My years of service spanned decades. I served in the United States Marine Corps from 1988 to 1992 as a Military Police officer, rising to roles such as Desk Sergeant, Acting Watch Commander, and Convoy Commander. Later, I continued my service in the U.S. Navy Reserves from 1999 to 2019 as a Logistics Specialist and Lead Petty Officer, deploying overseas and serving in leadership roles, including as a Forward Deployed Chaplain Representative.

In civilian life, I served with the El Paso County Sheriff's Department from 2005 to 2013, working as a detention officer, gang intelligence officer, and ceremonial commander. I later became a United States Border Patrol Agent from 2013 to 2021, where I also served as a chaplain, resiliency program manager, and Veteran Support Program Field Coordinator. Today, I continue that mission as a Mission Support Specialist and chaplain.

Through all of it, my motivation remained the same: to serve others. To share knowledge. To give back. I always believed that knowledge does no good if it is kept to yourself.

But service comes with a cost—one that most people never see.

There were moments during my deployments that left a lasting impact on me—moments of helplessness while following orders that either caused harm or prevented us from helping those in need. There were operations boarding foreign vessels, where small teams of five to seven of us would search ships carrying thirty or more personnel. We moved through massive ships—sometimes up to 900 feet long—often blind, not knowing what was around the next corner. The uncertainty was constant.

Spiritually, I also faced challenges. Being surrounded by environments where different beliefs dominated, I could feel a kind of spiritual oppression that I didn't yet fully understand.

For years, I carried all of this without realizing what it was doing to me.

It wasn't until 2014, after my last deployment, that everything came to the surface. I was driving with my wife and children when a vehicle suddenly cut me off. It looked like the vehicles I had encountered overseas—ragged, unpredictable. In an instant, I wasn't in Texas anymore—I was back in the Middle East. My training took over. I reacted as if I were in a convoy, assigned as a blocker. Without thinking, I forced the vehicle out of the way. That moment shook me. It was the first time I realized something was wrong.

What followed were symptoms I couldn't ignore—anger, anxiety, hypervigilance, insomnia, and nightmares. But what hurt the most was how it affected my family. My wife and children bore the weight of reactions I didn't understand. I thought I had anger issues, but in reality, it was PTSD. I just didn't know it yet.

I felt out of control—like I didn't recognize myself anymore. I didn't understand what was happening inside me, and that isolation made it even worse.

I didn't turn to alcohol or drugs, but I coped in my own way. I buried myself in work. Overtime. More deployments. I found peace in the chaos because silence was harder to face. Yet even in those quiet moments, I found myself reaching out to God— seeking guidance, even when I didn't fully understand Him.

Before coming to Christ, my view of God was distant and distorted. During my time in the Marine Corps, I saw Him as uncaring—as if He were watching my struggles from a distance. I was angry.

Everything changed about two years after leaving the Marines. My wife invited me to church, and during one service, the pastor shared a story about a Marine who had been bullied. As he spoke, he described actions, attitudes, and behaviors that hit close to home. The message was about pride—the difference between man-made identity and God-made identity.

In that moment, I realized something hard: I wasn't the victim in the story. I was the aggressor, I was the bully.

God spoke directly into my life that day. The pastor didn't know me or my past—but God did. And He met me right where I was. That day, something broke inside me—in a good way.

God broke the chains of pride. Machismo. Marine pride. That lone-wolf mentality I had carried for years. He showed me that I was never meant to do life alone.

From that moment on, everything began to change. My relationship with Christ became personal. Prayer was no longer a ritual—it became a conversation. I could bring my struggles to Him, and through His Word, He would answer me, often in ways that lifted me up exactly when I needed it.

My identity shifted—from someone who expected to be served to someone called to serve. I went from believing the world owed me something to understanding that I was called to give, to lead, and to love as Christ did.

The healing didn't happen overnight—and it still continues today. The memories are still there. The feelings don't completely disappear. But now I face them differently. Through Christ, I have strength. As Scripture says, I can do all things through Him who strengthens me.

Today, my life is centered on becoming more like Christ. It's not easy. Every day brings challenges—but also victories. I've learned to fall forward into God instead of falling backward into old habits. That shift took years, but it changed everything.

I stay disciplined—not just physically, but spiritually. Where I once trained my body, I now train my mind and spirit through prayer, Scripture, and seeking God daily.

I also make it a priority to help others. I make myself available to fellow veterans and first responders who are struggling, because I know what that darkness feels like.

If I could say one thing to anyone battling PTSD, it would be this: You were never meant to fight this battle alone. Just like in the military or law enforcement, we fight as a team. Healing works the same way. Seek God. Seek someone who will walk alongside you. That first step matters.

And if you feel alone—find a community. Find a church that teaches God's Word with truth and love. The fear of being judged is real, but true community brings healing, not condemnation.

If you are considering giving your life to Christ, keep it simple. You've tried other ways. Other solutions. Other people. But there is One who has already laid down His life for you. His name is Jesus.

In the military, we train for battle without knowing the outcome. But in God's army, the outcome is already decided. He wins. And because He wins, so do we.

The Cost of THE CALL
Finding Healing from PTSD in Christ

As 2 Timothy 2:3 reminds us, "You therefore must endure hardship as a good soldier of Jesus Christ." We are not alone in this fight. And as Matthew 20:26 teaches, true greatness comes through serving others.

One day, when this life is over, I know where I'm going. Not standing guard—but walking in victory.

Until then, I will continue to fight—this time, with Christ leading the way.

Eloy Zaragoza
United States Marine Corps Veteran (1988-1992), United States Navy Reserve (1999-2019), El Paso County Sheriff's Department (2005 – 2013), US Border Patrol Agent (2013-2022). Currently, I'm serving as a Chaplain.

INTRODUCTION TO TESTIMONY TWO

Many veterans and first responders struggle most after the mission ends. When the uniform comes off, the structure, identity, and camaraderie that once defined daily life can suddenly disappear. What remains are memories, questions, and sometimes a deep sense of isolation. This testimony speaks to that difficult transition and the way faith can provide a new foundation when the old one fades.

Testimony two

I was born in Rio de Janeiro, Brazil, and moved to the United

States when I was four years old. We settled in the Bay Area, in Oakland, California. I grew up in a strong but structured household. My parents were immigrants, each carrying a unique and complex background that shaped our family life.

My father was born in Shanghai, China, of Chinese and Portuguese descent—what is known as Macanese. My mother was Brazilian, with a rich heritage that included Indigenous Brazilian, African, German, and Danish roots. It was a rare and beautiful combination of cultures, but also one shaped by hardship. Both of my parents had difficult childhoods. My father lost both of his parents at the age of ten, and my mother was placed in a convent at nine years old after her parents divorced. In many ways, they grew up as orphans.

Because of their experiences, our home was strict. They carried different upbringings but were united in one thing— their Catholic faith, even though it was practiced in different ways. Discipline, structure, and survival were deeply ingrained in our household.

As a young man, I dreamed of seeing the world. I wanted to visit the countries my parents came from and experience life beyond Oakland. I was drawn to the sea and aspired to become a Merchant Marine. That desire eventually led me to join the United States Navy, following the path of many of my cousins—but also as a way to create a different life for myself.

The Cost of THE CALL
Finding Healing from PTSD in Christ

I served in the U.S. Navy for over twenty years. My primary role was as an aviation storekeeper, but I quickly became known as someone who could do just about anything. I took on numerous responsibilities—funeral details, honor guard, color guard, equipment operator. If it had wheels or controls, I could operate it. From trucks and forklifts to tugs and lifts, I embraced every opportunity to learn.

Looking back, I truly believe God had His hand on me, even when I did not fully recognize it. There is no way I could have accomplished all that I did on my own. Over the course of my career, I wore many hats. At one point, I even served in roles typically reserved for officers, despite being enlisted.

Because I joined at the age of twenty-four, I was considered "older" than most recruits. That earned me the nickname "The Old Man"—a name that stuck with me throughout my entire career, even among senior leadership. Along the way, I became more than just a service member. I became a counselor, a mentor, a leader—what many would call a "sea daddy." I helped guide younger sailors through their own struggles, often while silently battling my own.

Service came with a cost. Over the years, I experienced things that left a lasting impact on my mind and heart. I witnessed death—bodies floating in the water, victims of accidents covered in blood. I participated in funeral honors, burying service members and civilians alike. I stood before grieving families, delivering devastating news, and endured their cries, their anger, and their heartbreak.

One of the most difficult moments in my life was holding a close friend as he died in my arms. That moment alone left a deep wound that would follow me for years.

To cope, I turned to alcohol. It became my escape—from the pain, from the memories, from the long hours and the loneliness of being away from home. That lifestyle eventually led to two failed marriages. I was functioning on the outside, but internally I was unraveling.

Deep down, I knew something was wrong. But where I came from, you did not talk about your feelings—you buried them. You pushed forward. You handled it on your own. So I masked the pain the only way I knew how—through work and alcohol.

I struggled with anger, anxiety, depression, hypertension, and insomnia. PTSD quietly took control of areas of my life without me even realizing it. It damaged my relationships, cost me friendships, and turned me into someone who was constantly working or drinking just to avoid facing reality.

There were times at family gatherings when I would simply disappear—physically present one moment, gone the next. I was disconnected, isolated, and convinced that no one could understand the battle going on inside me.

Before truly surrendering to Christ, I kept God at a distance. I did not think He needed to be involved in my problems. I believed I could handle everything on my own. After all, that is how I was raised—if you make a mistake, you deal with it yourself. You do not burden others with your struggles.

Alcohol and partying became my coping mechanisms. I did not want God interfering in my life because I thought I had control. The truth was, I did not.

Everything changed when I gave my life to Jesus Christ. It was the greatest decision I have ever made.

My wife, Bel, played a huge role in that transformation. She is a strong Christian woman who has stood by me for over twenty-two years. Her faith, her prayers, and her unwavering commitment to God were instrumental in leading me to Christ. I know my mother was praying for me as well.

Through their prayers and God's grace, my heart began to change. When I finally surrendered, I experienced something I had never known before—forgiveness. It felt like a massive burden had been lifted off my shoulders. The joy I experienced is hard to put into words. To know that a holy and powerful God could forgive someone like me—and continue to love me despite my imperfections—was overwhelming.

My healing journey has not been easy. Even after giving my life to Christ, the battle did not disappear overnight. It has been a process—one that continues to this day. But now, I no longer fight alone.

Prayer, fasting, fellowship, and the support of strong Christian brothers have become essential in my life. Men like my brother Eloy, Captain Ron, and many others have stood with me in prayer and encouragement. I have learned to rely on the tools God has given us—the Holy Spirit, His Word, the armor of God, and a community of believers.

One of the Scriptures that has anchored me is:

"Rejoice always, pray continually, give thanks in all circumstances; for this is God's will for you in Christ Jesus" (1 Thessalonians 5:16–18).

That verse has carried me through some of my darkest moments.

Today, my life is no longer a blur. I have clarity, purpose, and peace that I never had before. Christ has transformed me into a more loving, patient, and understanding person. I still carry regrets for the people I have hurt along the way, but now I strive to make a difference by mentoring others—especially the younger generation in my family and anyone God places in my path.

My goal is simple: to lead others to God and share what He has done in my life.

To any veteran or first responder struggling with PTSD, I

want to tell you this: you are not alone, and there is hope.

The Bible says, *"Greater is He who is in you than he who is in the world"* (1 John 4:4). That truth has sustained me. And in my darkest moments, I hold on to this promise:

"Even though I walk through the valley of the shadow of death, I will fear no evil, for You are with me" (Psalm 23:4).

God has never left me, and He will not leave you.

If He can save and restore someone like me, He can do the same for you. When you surrender your life to Jesus, the burden you have been carrying begins to lift. You may not be able to fully explain it—but you will experience it.

And when you do, you will know: healing is real, hope is alive, and you were never meant to fight this battle alone.

HAJ "Uncle Ricky "de Sousa

United States Navy 1985-2005, CBP Mission Support 2009-2022. Currently, I am serving as a safety/security team member and other curricular that comes up at my church, PVC Mission.

INTRODUCTION TO TESTIMONY THREE

For some, the breaking point comes unexpectedly. A moment, an event, or a season of life exposes wounds that have been buried for years. It is often in those moments of vulnerability that a person begins searching for something deeper than temporary solutions. The testimony you are about to read reflects that journey from brokenness toward hope.

Testimony three

I was born on March 11, 1979, and raised in a small town called Raymondville, Texas. I grew up dirt poor, in a broken home where survival was more familiar than stability. My mom worked constantly just to keep us afloat, and even with everything on her shoulders, she still tried to take us to church whenever she could. But outside of those moments, everything around us was chaos.

Drugs and alcohol were a normal part of family life. Every aunt, uncle, and cousin seemed caught up in it. Family gatherings were unpredictable—you just knew that before the night was over, someone was going to fight. As strange as it sounds, I grew up expecting it… even looking forward to it. That kind of environment shapes you in ways you don't realize until much later.

We did go to church. My mom was a Sunday school teacher, and we were there multiple times a week. But even with that foundation, our home was still broken. My dad never went to church. He was an alcoholic who cheated on and abused my mom. As a kid, I didn't know any different—I thought that was normal.

Growing up, I didn't have dreams or goals. College was

never something we talked about. The military wasn't even on my radar. When I graduated high school, instead of feeling excited, I fell into a deep depression. I didn't know what came next. I didn't know what my life was supposed to be.

After bouncing between a few jobs, I ended up in Georgia working at a factory. I was nineteen years old and felt completely stuck—like my life had no direction and no purpose. Then one day, everything changed.

I went to a junkyard with a friend to help translate for him, and that's when I saw a man wearing a sharp uniform. He stood out immediately. He carried himself differently. I later found out he was a Marine recruiter—the son of the junkyard owner. I asked him for his card and told him I was thinking about joining.

He looked at me and asked, "Are you okay? Are you in trouble? Why do you want to join?"

I told him the truth: my life wasn't going anywhere, and I needed purpose.

Three to four weeks later, I was standing on the yellow footprints at Parris Island, beginning Marine Corps boot camp.

Life in the Marine Corps was both hard and simple at the same time. It took time to adjust to the discipline, the structure, and constantly being told what to do. But there was something about it that made sense. You either learned and moved forward, or you fell behind. There was no in-between.

I served primarily in satellite communications and as a field radio operator—the guy carrying the radio on his back. Our mission was to ensure communication, no matter the conditions.

Then, about a year and a half into my service, everything changed. 9/11 happened.

That day shifted the course of our lives. Shortly after, I was deployed to the Horn of Africa, and the war on terrorism began. I found myself in places most people only hear about—Djibouti, Islamabad, Afghanistan, Bahrain, and other regions across the Middle East.

I was only twenty-one, maybe twenty-two years old, and I was experiencing things no young man should have to process. What I saw and lived through overseas left a mark on me—mentally, emotionally, and spiritually.

I remember being at an embassy in Africa when I suddenly couldn't catch my breath. I thought something was seriously wrong. I went to a Navy corpsman, and he told me it was probably indigestion—told me to take some Tums and move on. So, I did. I pushed through, just like we were trained to do.

Near the end of my four-year contract, something unexpected happened—my girlfriend, who is now my wife, came back into my life after three years. We reconnected, got together, and started building a life. From the outside, everything looked fine. But on the inside, I was falling apart.

I was dealing with PTSD, anxiety, depression, and panic attacks—but I didn't know how to explain it, and I didn't want anyone to see it. I became an alcoholic and spent ten years hiding my struggles from my wife.

Eventually, I couldn't hide it anymore. I went to the VA for help, and they put me on medication. But the meds didn't fix what was going on inside. I became extremely hypervigilant. Crowded places triggered panic attacks. High-traffic areas made me feel like I was back overseas. So I started isolating. I stayed home. I withdrew from everything—and everyone. And that isolation began to damage my relationship with my family.

Before Christ, my life was in pieces. I was angry—not just at God, but at everything. I didn't know how to fix what was broken inside me. But God had a plan. And it started with my wife.

She prayed for me. Consistently. Faithfully. Even when I pushed back. Even when I argued with her about going to church. I fought her on it, but she never gave up.

I can't point to one dramatic moment where everything changed overnight. For me, it was a process. God worked on me little by little. Slowly breaking down walls I didn't even know I had built. Before I knew it, I was all in. God transformed my life.

I went from being a man controlled by alcohol and broken by PTSD to a man who fears God, loves his family, and finds peace in Christ. Today, my life looks completely different.

That doesn't mean the trials are gone. They're not. Challenges still come. There are still moments that test me. But now I know I'm not facing them alone. I know who walks with me through every situation.

Even when I don't understand what I'm going through, I trust that God is using it to shape me into the man He's called me to be.

If you're struggling with PTSD, hear this clearly:

You are not alone.

Find a church. Get connected. There are other veterans and first responders who understand exactly what you're going through. You don't have to carry this by yourself.

As Scripture says, "I can do all things through Christ who strengthens me" (Philippians 4:13).

Put your trust in Him. He will carry you through.

M. Chavarría
United States Marine Corps Veteran (1999–2003).
Currently, serving in security ministry at LMC.

INTRODUCTION TO TESTIMONY FOUR

The Cost of THE CALL
Finding Healing from PTSD in Christ

One of the most powerful truths about redemption is that God often transforms the very pain that once threatened to destroy us into something that helps others. The following testimony reflects that transformation—a life that has been reshaped by faith and now serves as a source of encouragement for those still walking through the battle.

Testimony four

I grew up in Edinburg, Texas, but my childhood wasn't rooted in one place. We moved around often, even living in Michigan and Minnesota for a time. I stayed at my grandparents' house for a while, then with my uncle, and eventually we settled into what became our final home when I reached middle school.

When I think back on my early years, I remember both joy and tension. As a family, we spent a lot of time together—playing outside, going for walks at UTPA, and enjoying the simple things. But as I got older, things began to change. We stopped going out as much, and my parents began drinking more frequently. That shift created a heaviness in our home. What once felt warm slowly became tense and unpredictable.

Faith, however, was always present—at least through my mom.

She was the only spiritual example I had growing up. She would tell us Bible stories on the way to school; my favorite memory was seeing her wake up early to pray. At night, she would pray with my siblings and me, and even after we went to bed, she would continue praying on her own. Those moments stayed with me, even when I didn't fully understand them.

As a child, I dreamed of becoming a lawyer. I was fascinated by what I saw on television—the arguments, the strategy, the excitement. I wanted a life that felt meaningful and engaging.

But everything changed after I read a book called *Ghosts of War* by Ryan Smithson. That book shifted something inside me. For the first time, I felt drawn toward military service. After speaking with recruiters and instructors in JROTC, I realized the Navy felt like the right path for me.

I joined the United States Navy and began serving as a logistics specialist. My roles varied—I worked as a postal clerk, a customer service representative, and even spent time working in the galley. At first, my motivation was simple: I wanted to be part of something bigger than myself. Later, that motivation deepened. My children became my reason. I wanted to show them that hard work, discipline, and perseverance could come from anyone, regardless of where they started.

But service came with a cost.

One of the hardest realities of military life was time away

from home. I missed some of the most important milestones in my children's lives. I was gone for long stretches—sometimes over a year and a half with only brief visits in between. I would come home for a weekend, only to leave again for weeks. That constant separation took a toll on me emotionally, even if I didn't fully recognize it at the time.

Then came a season that would change everything.

In 2020, my husband and I found out we were expecting a baby. It should have been one of the happiest times in my life, but instead, it became one of the most overwhelming. At the same time, I was taking a course to address my struggles with alcohol. We were in the middle of moving into a new apartment when we received sudden news—my husband had five days to get his affairs in order before deploying.

I was not prepared.

I had never truly been alone before, and the thought terrified me. My family couldn't afford to visit, and I didn't have close friends nearby. At work, things weren't any easier. I had been placed in charge of my shop, even though I didn't have the rank others did. That created tension. Some people didn't respect my position, and I found myself constantly trying to prove myself while already feeling overwhelmed.

Then one night, everything escalated.

As I was heading to my apartment, I noticed two men

attempting to break in. By God's grace, I saw them before I got too close and was able to call the police in time. But that moment shook me deeply.

After that, fear took over.

I developed anxiety and depression that quickly spiraled into something deeper. I stopped taking care of myself. My home became a reflection of what I was feeling inside—neglected, chaotic, and heavy. At night, I would lie awake, overwhelmed, praying that God would just take me. I felt like I was doing life wrong, like I wasn't worthy of living it anymore.

The fear didn't stay in one place—it followed me everywhere.

I became paranoid. I stopped going out in public. I avoided people. At work and even at appointments, I would constantly look for exits. I checked locks repeatedly. I felt like I was always in danger, even when I was safe.

I didn't recognize myself anymore.

I became quiet. I avoided eye contact. I felt unworthy and completely alone—even in rooms full of people. I tried to hide it by telling others it was just pregnancy-related stress, but inside, I felt like I was slowly dying.

I wasn't eating. I wasn't sleeping. And I didn't want to live.

Before Christ, my relationship with God was distant. I knew He could hear me, but I didn't feel close to Him. I didn't think

I deserved His attention. I didn't want to be a burden to Him.

Yet even in that darkness, God was still working.

I believe one of the reasons I held on was because of my son. I knew God had given him to me for a reason, and even when I didn't want to live, I knew I needed to be there for him.

My turning point didn't come in a single dramatic moment—it came through people.

After leaving the military and stepping away from the lifestyle of drinking and partying, I began to feel an emptiness I couldn't ignore. I reconnected with friends from high school, and they invited me to church. They encouraged me, pushed me, and walked with me as I began to seek something more.

That's when I realized—I didn't just want to know about God, I wanted a relationship with Him.

Scripture began to speak into my life, especially Matthew 6:33–34. It reminded me that I didn't have to carry everything on my own. That I didn't need alcohol to survive—the Lord was going to help me.

For the first time in a long time, I felt something different.

I felt seen.

I felt heard.

I felt loved.

God began to change my heart.

Through my relationship with Christ, I started to understand my purpose. I realized I didn't have to live in fear anymore. Scriptures like 2 Timothy 1:7 reminded me that fear was not from God. With prayer, support from friends, and God's mercy, I began to overcome the paranoia that once controlled me.

My mindset began to shift.

Where there was once negativity, there was now hope. Where there was self-hatred, there was now love—not just for others, but for myself. I began to understand that I was never alone. God had been with me all along.

My healing is still ongoing.

I continue to battle with my past struggles, especially with alcohol. It's a daily choice—to choose God over what once numbed the pain. But I know that with Him, I have the strength to keep going.

Today, my life is different.

It's more peaceful, even in the chaos of raising two young boys. They are my blessing—my reminder of why I kept going. I now surround myself with people who draw me closer to God, not further away.

God has shifted my pace.

In the Navy, life was fast and demanding. Now, I am learning to slow down—to be present as a wife and a mother. I see my past not as something to be ashamed of, but as something God used to teach me how to depend fully on Him.

I now try to help others who are struggling—especially those dealing with loneliness. I reach out when I can and share what God has done in my life, hoping it will point someone else toward Him.

If you are struggling right now, hear this:

You are not alone.

God is with you, even when you don't feel Him. Call on the name of Jesus. Talk to Him. He hears you. He loves you. He is not distant.

And if you are considering giving your life to Christ—do it.

There is nothing greater than His love. It's not always easy, but it is worth it. The peace, the purpose, and the promise of eternal life with Him outweigh anything this world can offer.

In my darkest moments, God reminded me that He is my strength in weakness.

I don't need the world.

I have Him.

And He is more than enough.

H.H.

United States Navy Veteran (2018–2024)

INTRODUCTION TO TESTIMONY FIVE

Trauma does not always arrive in a single moment. Sometimes

it builds slowly, call after call, incident after incident, until the weight becomes difficult to carry. Many first responders and veterans silently shoulder that burden for years before anyone realizes what they are going through. The final testimony reveals what that hidden struggle can look like—and how God can step into even the most overwhelming seasons of life.

Testimony five

I was born in Matamoros, Tamaulipas, Mexico, though most of my upbringing took place in Texas. My mother was an American citizen, and my father was from Mexico. Because my father worked wherever he could find employment, we moved around frequently during my childhood. Houston became home during my early years, and later we relocated to Mission, Texas, around the time I was preparing to enter junior high school.

Growing up, I considered our family fairly normal. I was the oldest of four children, and like most brothers, we fought over silly things—the television remote, food, or making fun of one another. My father worked constantly, so we usually only saw him on weekends. My mother stayed home and took care of us. She made sure we did our homework and kept us disciplined. If needed, she wasn't afraid to grab a belt or sandal to keep us in line.

Faith was present in our home, though not perfectly. My father believed in God but did not care much for church. My mother, however, made sure we learned about Him. She would take us to a Baptist church from time to time and taught us Bible verses like John 3:16. Looking back now, I realize she was planting seeds in us that would later matter more than I understood at the time.

As a kid, my dreams changed often. One day I wanted to be a pilot after watching *Airwolf* and *Top Gun*. Other days I wanted to be in law enforcement like *Walker, Texas Ranger*, fighting bad guys and protecting people. I had dreams, but no real direction. Even after high school, I still did not know what I wanted to do with my life.

I tried college because it was something my mother wanted for me before she passed away, but I lacked focus. I enjoyed working with my hands more than sitting in classrooms. Construction became my trade. I worked alongside my father and uncle in the drywall business throughout my twenties, trying to build something for myself and help support the family.

Then life changed.

The housing market collapsed, construction work disappeared, and my business failed. I found myself in a difficult place financially and emotionally. I did not know where to go from there. One day, while talking with my barber—an Air Force veteran—he encouraged me to consider military service. His words reminded me of something a schoolteacher once told us: "If you ever find yourself in a rough spot and things don't go your way, you can always join the military."

So that is exactly what I did.

At thirty-three years old, I enlisted in the United States Army during a time of war.

Most of my family had served in the Marine Corps, but after hearing stories from my brother about the difficulty of Marine training—and especially the swimming requirements—I decided the Army would be a better fit for me. Ironically, despite being a weak swimmer, I eventually became a bridge crewmember, boat operator, and HEMTT truck driver.

I chose MOS 21C, Bridge Crewmember, because of my construction background. Our mission involved building bridges and transporting military personnel and supplies across the Euphrates River in Iraq. We also trained alongside combat engineers using explosives in case we ever needed to destroy bridges to prevent enemy advances.

The attacks on September 11, 2001, played a major role in my decision to serve. Like many Americans, I felt called to defend my country and protect my family. I also hoped the military would give me direction and purpose.

What most people do not understand about wartime service is the constant awareness that death could come at any moment.

Our company motto was, "Stay Alert, Stay Alive." That was not just a slogan—it was reality. Every mission carried danger. We constantly watched for IEDs, snipers, suicide bombers, and mortar attacks. Our bridge missions often placed us in open, exposed areas, making us high-risk targets.

But the deepest wounds I carried did not begin in Iraq.

Before deployment, my mother died from cancer.

As a young Christian, I truly believed God would heal her. I clung to Scriptures about faith and healing. Our church prayed for her constantly, and I believed with all my heart that God would intervene. Then one day my father called from the hospital, and I heard my grandmother screaming and crying: "Your mother just died!"

I was devastated.

My faith shattered in that moment. I questioned everything. Why would God allow this? Why did He not answer our prayers? I searched the Bible desperately for answers and attended grief counseling groups trying to understand the "why" behind my pain, but nothing seemed to satisfy the emptiness I felt inside.

Then came Iraq.

On August 4, 2006, while stationed at Camp Habbaniyah, our Humvee rolled over during a mission near the Euphrates River. Another vehicle approached us unexpectedly, and our driver swerved to avoid a collision. The Humvee was fully armored and extremely heavy. Once it tipped, it rolled multiple times.

During the rollover, my left foot was crushed. I remember being thrown outside the vehicle, lying on the ground in pain, trying to remove my vest and locate my weapon. I could hear chaos around me—voices shouting, soldiers calling for a medevac.

Then I heard Sergeant Segura struggling to breathe.

He had been crushed in the turret during the rollover. I remember hearing another soldier performing CPR while desperately calling for help.

A Blackhawk helicopter eventually arrived and transported him away. I was flown to Landstuhl Regional Medical Center in Germany for surgery. My injuries were serious but not life-threatening.

Weeks later, I learned Sergeant Segura had died that day.

That news haunted me.

After leaving the Army, I drove to his gravesite in Fort Sumner, New Mexico. I stood there, saluted him, and cried. I carried survivor's guilt for years.

"Lord, why him and not me?"

That question replayed in my mind constantly.

Eventually, I began noticing symptoms I could no longer ignore. During an MRI scan years later, the sounds inside the machine triggered overwhelming panic. I felt trapped and helpless. I had to leave the clinic and broke down crying outside.

Driving became another trigger. Whenever someone else was behind the wheel, especially if they were distracted, my anxiety skyrocketed. My mind immediately went into survival mode, planning escape routes and preparing for disaster.

PTSD slowly isolated me from people.

Before the military, I enjoyed spending time with family and friends. After Iraq, I preferred being alone. I withdrew emotionally and socially. I gained weight from comfort eating and became ashamed of my appearance. Alcohol also became a temporary escape, but instead of numbing the memories, it replayed them over and over in my mind like an endless loop.

Even through all of this, I never completely stopped believing in God.

In the hospital, I watched wounded veterans arrive with injuries far worse than mine. Some screamed in their sleep. Others cried openly. All I could do was pray.

My mother's death had shaken my faith deeply, but the trauma from Iraq slowly pushed me back toward God. Not immediately—but little by little. Like a moth drawn toward a light.

There were moments when anger and confusion consumed me. I questioned why God spared me. Why was I still alive? What purpose could there possibly be for someone missing a foot and carrying so much pain?

Yet even during those seasons, God was still pursuing me.

Years earlier, during a summer trip to my father's ranch in Mexico, God had already begun working on my heart. I did not want to be there. There was no electricity, no entertainment, and as a teenager I was bored out of my mind.

One night, while listening to an AM radio station in my father's van, I discovered a Christian radio program called *Unshackled*. The show shared testimonies of transformed lives. Night after night, I listened.

Something inside me began to change.

I remember praying, "God, I want what these people have. I want my life transformed."

That was the moment I truly surrendered my life to Christ.

I felt the Holy Spirit fill my heart. God's presence became so real to me that after praying, I almost expected to physically see Him standing beside me. For the first time, I understood

His love personally.

Over the years, God continued healing me through His presence, His Word, and my family.

My wife Charlene stood faithfully beside me after I lost my foot. Together we raised our son, Ozzie, and our daughter, Amelia. My life was no longer centered on my pain or disability. I had people to love and responsibilities that mattered.

Psalm 118:17–18 became deeply meaningful to me:

"I shall not die, but live, and declare the works of the Lord. The Lord has chastened me severely, but He has not given me over to death."

I still do not fully understand why God allowed certain things to happen. But I know this: He did not abandon me.

Today, the trauma no longer controls my identity.

I am not just a wounded soldier living in survival mode. I am a child of God walking one day at a time with Christ.

Healing is still ongoing, especially physically. Phantom pain from my amputation remains, and certain memories still surface during moments like Memorial Day. But God continues giving me strength.

Today I work part-time at AutoZone, not because I have to, but because it helps me stay active and connected with people. My family attends church faithfully, and I serve on our church

The Cost of THE CALL
Finding Healing from PTSD in Christ

security team.

If I could say one thing to veterans and first responders battling PTSD, it would be this:

God is the answer.

It may not feel that way at first, but He truly is. Support groups and counseling can help, but ultimately, real peace comes from Christ.

This battle is not only physical or psychological—it is spiritual.

The enemy wants us trapped in fear, guilt, anger, and isolation. But God fights for us.

Exodus 14:14 says, "The Lord will fight for you; you need only to be still."

You are not alone. You are still needed.

And if you give your life fully to Christ, you will never regret it.

The military offers brotherhood, but Christ offers something even greater—eternal purpose.

This is no longer just a physical battle.

It is a spiritual one.

And with the armor of God, we can stand.

Rodolfo "Rudy" Rodriguez
U.S. Army Veteran (2005 – 2008)
Church security team

FINAL WORDS

The Battle Is Not the End

If you have walked through the pages of this book, then you already know something about the battles many veterans and first responders face. Some of those battles happen in dangerous places, in the chaos of emergencies or the uncertainty of combat. Others take place quietly, inside the mind and the heart, long after the mission has ended.

The truth is that many people never see those internal battles.

They see the uniform. They see the professionalism. They see the courage displayed in moments of crisis. What they do not always see are the sleepless nights, the memories that refuse to fade, the silent questions, and the moments when hope feels distant.

Yet throughout this book we have seen a powerful truth emerge: the battle does not have to define the ending of the story.

Again and again, Scripture reminds us that God does some of His greatest work in places of struggle. Moses met God in the wilderness. David discovered his calling while hiding in caves. Elijah heard the voice of God not in the storm, but in the quiet whisper that followed.

Even the Apostle Paul, who endured hardship, imprisonment, and suffering, declared in 2 Corinthians 12:9 that God's grace is sufficient and that His power is made perfect in weakness. The same truth applies to us today.

Pain may shape our journey, but it does not have to steal our purpose. Trauma may leave scars, but those scars can become reminders of God's faithfulness and instruments through which others find hope.

Many of the testimonies you have read in this book prove that redemption is real.

Christ does not wait for people to become perfect before reaching them. He meets them in their struggles, in their questions, and sometimes in the darkest moments of their lives. From that place of brokenness, He begins a work of restoration that unfolds one step at a time.

Healing rarely happens overnight. It often comes slowly— through prayer, through community, through honest conversations, and through the steady presence of God in everyday life. But healing is possible.

If you are reading this book while fighting your own internal battle, remember this: you are not alone, and your story is not finished.

The same God who walked with these men through their darkest seasons is still present today. He still calls people out of despair and into hope. He still restores what seems broken and gives purpose to what once felt meaningless.

Your past may be part of your story, but it does not have to be the final chapter.

Through Christ, even the deepest wounds can become part of a testimony that points others toward healing, redemption, and faith.

And sometimes, the greatest victories are not the battles we win in the field, but the ones we win in the heart.

He is not finished with you yet... "For we are his workmanship, created in Christ Jesus for good works, which God prepared beforehand, that we should walk in them."

EPHESIANS 2:10

About The Author

David Mendoza III is a dedicated servant leader with a rich tapestry of experience spanning faith, service, and storytelling. Holding a seminary degree in biblical studies, he brings a deep understanding of faith and scripture to his work. A retired federal law enforcement officer with over thirty years of service, David has dedicated his life to protecting and serving others. His military background as a Marine Corps veteran further underscores his commitment to duty and resilience.

David's passion for helping others extends beyond his professional life. He has served as a law enforcement chaplain, a peer support member, and a Veterans Support Program volunteer, offering guidance and support to those in need. Currently, David is a Christian minister and former pastor, sharing his faith and wisdom through his ministry.

He is also the author of several award-winning books, including *Unleashed Redemption, The King & His Bride, Jed's Journal* and a variety of children's titles, all of which bring biblical narratives to life for the entire family.

David's life is a testament to the power of faith, service, and storytelling. He is a devoted husband of over thirty years, a father of two boys, and an active member of his church community, where he and his wife are deeply involved in adult and children's ministry, serving as Sunday school teachers, Royal Rangers Commanders, and home Bible group leaders. David's unwavering commitment to helping others, sharing his testimony, and offering support during times of need makes him a true inspiration.

David is reachable via email at *authordavidmendozaiii@yahoo.com* or you can visit his website at *www.booksforhisglory.com* to get in touch.